Belarski

PULP ART MASTERS

ADVENTURE HOUSE

**WRITTEN AND DESIGNED
BY JOHN P. GUNNISON
SILVER SPRING, MD**

Dedication:
To Rudolph Belarski. If not for his great talent and all those pulp publishers, this book would have never been produced.

Adventure House is dedicated to bringing the "pulp era" to the public. Fantastic images and prose were commonplace among the great pulp masters.

Acknowledgements: This book could not have been completed without the limitless talents of Doug Ellis, John Locke, Frank Robinson and particularly Tom Roberts.

Library of Congress Cataloging-in-Publication Data
Gunnison, John 1955 —
        Belarski: Pulp art masters / John Gunnison
        p.   cm.
        Includes bibliographical references and index.
        Contents: Historical overview of pulp cover art.
ISBN 1-886937-76-1 (pbk)
        1. Magazine covers—United States. I. Gunnison, John II. Title.

2003090997
CIP

TABLE OF

CONTENTS

Adventure House
914 Laredo Road
Silver Spring, MD
20901-1867
301-754-1589
sales@adventurehouse.com
Sales catalogs available
upon request.

Adventure House
First Printing: July 2003

INTRODUCTION

✪ ✪ ✪ ✪ ✪

RUDOLPH BELARSKI'S artistic career began as a teen, with a simple illustration on a whitewashed wall at a Dupont, Pennsylvania coal processing plant. His duly impressed bosses set him to painting safety posters. After turning twenty-one he paid his way through the Pratt Institute in Brooklyn New York, a school particularly noted for fostering talented artists into commercial illustrators. Upon graduating, Belarski too embarked upon his career into the world of commercial art. But Pratt was not done with him just yet. The management at Pratt Institute was so impressed with the abilities he was demonstrating as a professional artist that in 1929, several years after he had graduated, Belarski was invited back to teach.

It was in the late 1920's, and the pulp magazines beckoned many young illustrators and Rudy Belarski heard their calling. The pulp-wood magazines had a voracious appetite for artwork, as news-stands were filled with provocative four-color covers. His first covers were destined for Dell's air pulps. With few exceptions, aviation covers dominated Belarski's easel until the mid-30's when he started painting covers for Ned Pines and the Thrilling Group of titles. Thrilling produced far more titles than Dell, and Rudolph Belarski was a key illustrator for both publishers.

Early in 1937 the Frank A. Munsey Company, publisher of **ARGOSY** and several detective titles, recruited Belarski even though he was still hard at work for Thrilling. Belarski accepted the offer but soon found himself taxed with the stress of too much work. It was during these busy times that Belarski would split his time between New York and cabins in Maine or Canada. While camping and relaxing from the hustle and bustle of city life, the artist painted covers in open sunlight of day sometimes polishing off a canvas and shipping it out in a cardboard box overnight.

During World War II, Belarski continued to work for Ned Pines and also entertained troops overseas in British hospitals with personal portraits. Between wartime paper shortages and the shrinking pulp market, Belarski made the partial jump to paperback covers for Pines' Popular Library. By late 1951 the jump to paperbacks was complete, as he forever left the ragged-edged pulpwood magazines behind.

This pictorial history of Rudolph Belarski's pulp covers is divided up into seven different chapters, ranging from adventure subjects through the weird menace field showcasing the wide range of his abilities. Rudy Belarski's eye for composition, his approach to action and use of color was rarely matched. Two decades have passed following his death, and more than three decade have come and gone since he last took up a brush to create a new image. Yet his covers still highly valued in the collectibles market, and avid collectors of both paperbacks and pulp magazine continue to seek out his work. This is no small testament to his substantial talents and abilities.

MACHINE GUNS AND MACHETES

✪ ✪ ✪ ✪ ✪

OF ALL the genres of pulp magazines, the adventure genre had one of the largest readerships. Titles like **ARGOSY, THRILLING ADVENTURES, ALL-AMERICAN FICTION** along with dozens of other adventure titles competed for the readers attention. Their fiction spanned from tales set against the background of ancient history to yarns with premises based upon a futuristic science. Characters from their pages sprang into our popular culture conscience, Tarzan, Dr. Kildare, Horatio Hornblower, John Carter of Mars, to name only a few crept into the lives of their readers and spawned new breeds of entertainment in the form of comic books, paperbacks and television.

Adventure fiction magazines changed their content over time to match the tastes of their readers. In the mid 30's, French Foreign Legionnaires fought and died in Saharan Africa; World War I doughboys bled in the trenches; and cannonballs shredded canvas sails fired by British Man O' Wars against rival nations. Some featured archaeologists discovering tombs, while the next would have Musketeers crossing swords on French soil. The horrors of real Europe hadn't invaded American shores and escape meant past adventures more than present conflicts. A not so subtle change in story and cover art occurred as Germany, Italy and Japan began their wars of conquest. Stories of Yellow Peril sprinkled with Nazi Spies dotted the pages and dominated the covers. Real war was soon to follow.

Belarski's cover illustrations ran the gamut as well. In his covers you could almost see the sweat forming on the brow of some explorer hacking through an African jungle, bullets tearing through the jodhpurs of some pith helmeted adventurer, or hear the swooshing of a sword swung by a Russian Cossack that is about to decapitate the reader. Working for both Munsey's **ARGOSY** and Pine's **THRILLING ADVENTURES**, Belarski brought to life many a dashing swashbuckler. As well as brought to life our fear of an inscrutable Japanese invader.

Although adventure fiction magazines were among the last to die out when the pulps faded into obscurity, Rudolph Belarski turned in his last canvases for **ARGOSY** and **THRILLING ADVENTURES** early on during World War II. For Belarski, his art was going to change course back to his past where he first got his start—in painting covers for the aviation magazines, this time illustrating British, Canadian and American aviators.

FRENCH FOREIGN LEGIONNAIRES

Image 1
ARGOSY
MAY 28 1938
The French Foreign Legion was a staple for ARGOSY, Belarski and Ted Roscoe.

Image 2
ARGOSY
JANUARY 22 1939
Edgar Rice Burroughs' name normally meant an increase in print run and sales.

Image 3
ALL-AMERICAN FICTION
OCTOBER 1938
All-American was a companion magazine to ARGOSY, but never really caught fire and was cancelled after a brief run.

MACHINE GUN MERCENARIES

Image 4
THRILLING ADVENTURES
SEPTEMBER 1936
Pith helmets and machine guns...a combination of a winning theme!

Image 5
ARGOSY
NOVEMBER 27 1937
Lester Dent was better known as Kenneth Robeson the author of Doc Savage.

Image 6
THRILLING ADVENTURES
JANUARY 1936
Hugh B. Cave is best known for his horror stories and is still a published author after seven decades of writing.

NOW 10¢ PER COPY

THRILLING ADVENTURES

SEPT.

NOW 10¢

FEATURING

RIVER OF DEATH
A Complete Novel of
New Guinea's Headhunters
By COLONEL
WILLIAM T.
COWIN

A THRILLING
PUBLICATION

GOLDEN HELL
An Amazing Icee Experience
By CAPTAIN HUMBERT REYNOLDS
•
THE DEVIL'S HOOF
A Novelette of Aleutian Piracy
By HERMAN HOWARD MATTESON

4

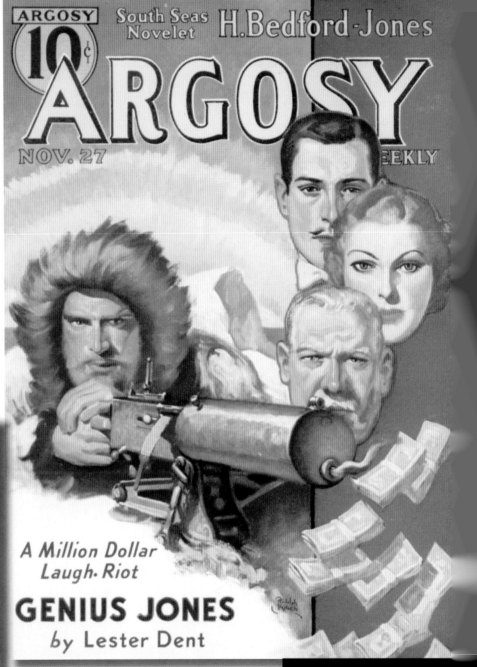

ARGOSY

South Seas Novelet H. Bedford-Jones

10¢

ARGOSY

NOV. 27   WEEKLY

*A Million Dollar
Laugh-Riot*

GENIUS JONES
by Lester Dent

5

ARMS FOR ETHIOPIA A Complete Action Novel

THRILLING ADVENTURES

JAN.

ALL
STORIES
COMPLETE

15¢

A THRILLING
PUBLICATION

THE GOLDEN NOOSE
A Complete Novelette
By LESLIE T. WHITE
•
HOLOCAUST HOUSE
By HUGH B. CAVE

6

ACTION ON EVERY PAGE!

THRILLING ADVENTURES

JAN.

NOW 10¢

A THRILLING PUBLICATION

Gunslingin' Galligan
By JOHNSTON McCULLEY

FEATURING
CURSE OF THE DEVIL DOCTOR
A Novelet of Burmese Terror
By E. HOFFMANN PRICE

ACTION THE WORLD OVER

THRILLING ADVENTURES

JULY

NOW 10¢

FEATURING
BURMA GUNS
A Novel of Jungle Conflict
By E. HOFFMANN PRICE

A THRILLING PUBLICATION

UNDERSEA RAIDERS
A Novelet of Today's War
By ROBERT SIDNEY BOWEN

7

8

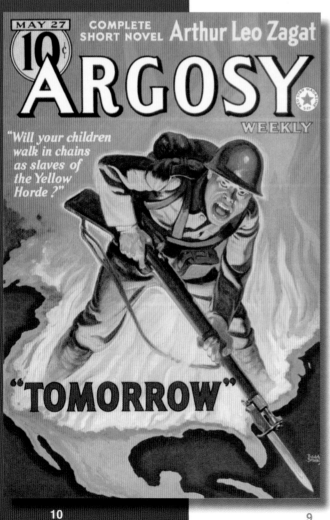

MAY 27

10¢

COMPLETE SHORT NOVEL   Arthur Leo Zagat

ARGOSY
WEEKLY

"Will your children walk in chains as slaves of the Yellow Horde?"

"TOMORROW"

ARGOSY

10¢

A Legion Novelet   Georges Surdez

ARGOSY
WEEKLY

AUG. 28

Mailed Fist Over America

Kingdom Come

W 42 BROADWAY

10

9

10

11

12

13

WAR IS HELL!

Image 7
THRILLING ADVENTURES JANUARY 1941
So now it's war! All war, whether imagined or not, was perfect grist for the pulp mill.

Image 8
THRILLING ADVENTURES JULY 1940
Since America wasn't at war, American pulp magazines had to feature Canadian and British soldiers.

Image 9
ARGOSY MAY 27 1939
For Americans, the "Yellow Peril" was a real threat. This story predates Pearl Harbor and was nearly prophetic of things to come.

Image 10
ARGOSY AUGUST 28 1937
The Nazi movement in the United States as envisioned by Rudolph Belarski.

Image 11
ARGOSY JUNE 4 1938
The faces of evil moving toward World War II.

Image 12
THRILLING ADVENTURES OCTOBER 1940
Lt. Scott Morgan was a house name that hid many a faceless writer for the "Thrilling Group."

Image 13
THRILLING ADVENTURES MARCH 1937
Before America came into World War II, stories that featured American soldiers normally had a Great War theme instead.

SPIES AND BLAZING GUNS

**Image 14
THRILLING
ADVENTURES
MARCH 1941**
The Allied Spy was seldom seen on covers, as the publishers seemed to prefer Axis spies.

**Image 15
THRILLING
ADVENTURES
SEPTEMBER 1940**
The author, Malcolm Wheeler-Nicholson, later became a pioneer in publishing comic books.

**Image 16
THRILLING
ADVENTURES
APRIL 1941**
Edgar Rice Burroughs at this time of his career was forced to find new pulp titles to publish his stories as his buying power was beginning to wane.

**Image 17
THRILLING
ADVENTURES
NOVEMBER 1943**
Louis L'Amour expanded his scope of story plots well beyond his western theme roots.

**Image 18
ARGOSY
SEPTEMBER 17 1938**
Horatio Hornblower sails along with adventure fan favorite, Talbot Mundy.

**Image 19
THRILLING
ADVENTURES
MAY 1936**
Foreign based adventures prior to World War II and eventually wartime cover themes.

14

15

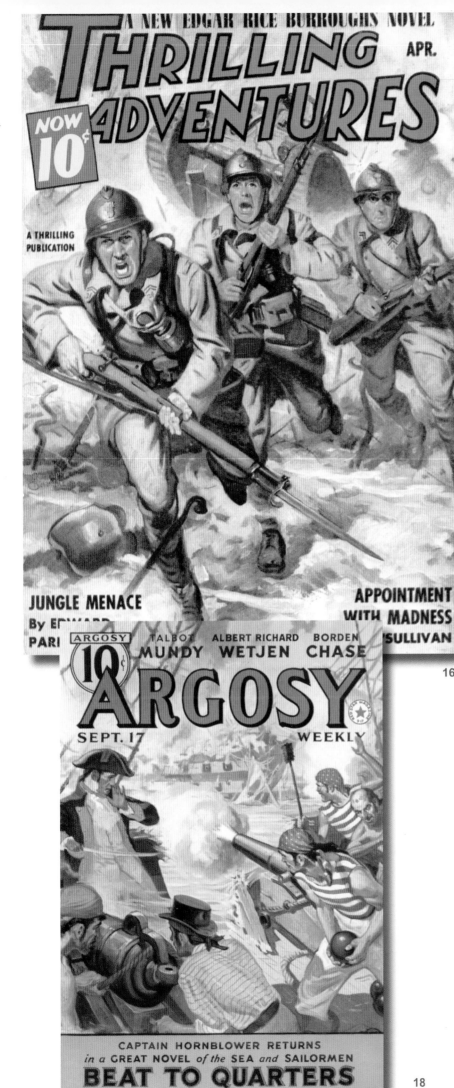

A NEW EDGAR RICE BURROUGHS NOVEL

THRILLING
APR.

NOW 10¢

ADVENTURES

A THRILLING
PUBLICATION

JUNGLE MENACE

By EDWARD
PAR...

APPOINTMENT
WITH MADNESS

...SULLIVAN

16

THRILLING
ADVENTURE

10¢

BLACK LACE
A Novelet of
The Spanish Main
By CARL JACOBI

W...
BR...
A P...
By
L'A...

17

ARGOSY

10¢

TALBOT   ALBERT RICHARD   BORDEN
MUNDY   WETJEN   CHASE

ARGOSY
SEPT. 17
WEEKLY

CAPTAIN HORNBLOWER RETURNS
in a GREAT NOVEL of the SEA and SAILORMEN
BEAT TO QUARTERS

18

NOW 10¢ PER COPY

THRILLING
MAY

NOW 10¢

ADVENTURES

ALL STORIES
COMPLETE

THE SQUADRON
OF FORGOTTEN
MEN
An Amazing
True
Experience
By CAPT.
HUGH
RANSOME

A THRILLING
PUBLICATION

THE
THIRTEEN
GATES
A Complete
Action Novel
By COLONEL
MARTIN GANPAT

COLOR
OF
GOLD
A
Complete
Novelette
By
WILLIAM
MERRIAM
ROUSE

19

ll STORIES mPLETE

ALL·American Fiction
JULY-AUG.
15¢

A Complete Novel
JOEL TOWNSLEY ROGERS

MAX BRAND · RICHARD SALE
H. BEDFORD-JONES
JAMES F. DWYER
DONALD BARR CHIDSEY

20

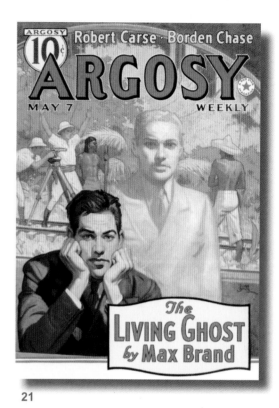

Robert Carse · Borden Chase

ARGOSY
10¢
MAY 7
WEEKLY

The
LIVING GHOST
by **Max Brand**

21

10¢ **Red ★ Star** JUNE
Adventures

*White Blood and Savage Cunning -- a Pagan's Strength
and a White Man's Courage -- They Called Him*
THE WHITE SAVAGE
And Every Rogue in the South Seas Feared His Name
A GREAT ADVENTURE NOVEL *by* MARTIN McCALL

22

ACTION THE WORLD OVER
THRILLING NOV.
ADVENTURES

NOW
10¢

A THRILLING
PUBLICATION

FEATURING
**CITY OF
BLOOD**
A Complete
Action Novel
By HENRY
KUTTNER

**PIECES
OF HATE**
A Story of
Buried Treasure
By REEVE WALKER

23

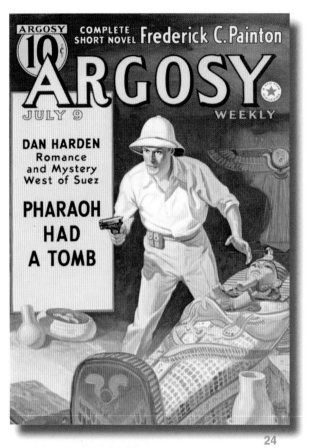

24

25

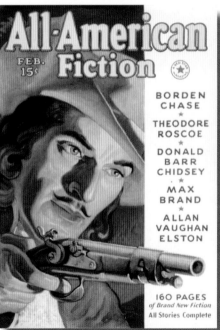

26

27

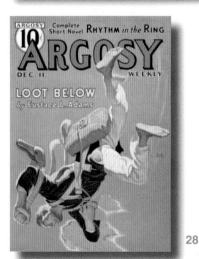

28

ADVENTURES
THROUGHOUT THE
AGES

Image 20
ALL-AMERICAN
FICTION
JULY-AUGUST 1938

Image 21
ARGOSY
MAY 7 1938
Max Brand was one of the
most prolific authors of all
time.

Image 22
RED STAR
ADVENTURES
JUNE 1940
A short lived series pro-
duced by the publisher of
ARGOSY.

Image 23
THRILLING
ADVENTURES
NOVEMBER 1940

Image 24
ARGOSY
JULY 9 1938
Ancient mummies and
romance?

Image 25
ARGOSY
JULY 17 1937
A solid background color
really sets off the tiger
and the treasure.

Image 26
ALL-AMERICAN
FICTION
FEBRUARY 1938
Theodore Roscoe, fea-
tured on the cover, was
best known for his French
Foreign Legion stories.

Image 27
THRILLING
ADVENTURES
DECEMBER 1936
Robert E. Howard, fea-
tured on the cover, was
the author of Conan the
Barbarian.

Image 28
ARGOSY
DECEMBER 11 1937
How about "Look Out
Below?"

15

29

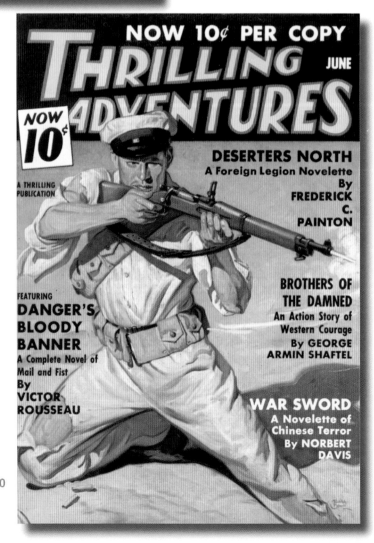

30

NOW 10¢ PER COPY

THRILLING ADVENTURES

JULY

NOW 10¢

ALL STORIES COMPLETE

A THRILLING PUBLICATION

FEATURING

THE HOUSE OF BAKRY BEY
A Novel of Mysterious Egypt
By ANTHONY PARSONS

GUNS BEFORE DAWN
A Western Novelette
By FORBES PARKHILL

YANKEE DOODLE
A Novelette of Bloody Strife
By WILLIAM MERRIAM ROUSE

31

10 NEW STORIES by FAMOUS AUTHORS

All-American Fiction

ALL STORIES COMPLETE

MAY-JUNE 15¢

MEET ME IN MIAMI
A Complete Short Novel

MAX BRAND
RICHARD SALE
H. BEDFORD-JONES
CORNELL WOOLRICH
EUSTACE COCKRELL
KARL DETZER

Adventure

Mystery

Romance

Action

32

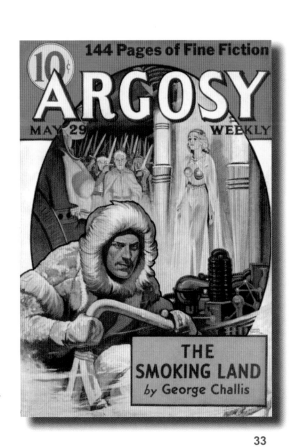

144 Pages of Fine Fiction

10¢

ARGOSY

MAY 29

WEEKLY

THE SMOKING LAND
by George Challis

33

THRILLING ADVENTURES

10¢

JULY

A THRILLING PUBLICATION

FEATURING

THE POISON PEOPLE
A Complete Thunder Jim Novel
By CHARLES STODDARD

WHITE RAIDER OF KENYA
An Action Novelet
By JOHN MacDOUGALL MURRAY

34

All-American Fiction
DEC.
15¢
ALL STAR

★ MAX BRAND ★ LUKE SHORT ★ RICHARD SALE
★ ROBERT CARSE ★ H. BEDFORD-JONES
★ FRANK RICHARDSON PIERCE
★ JOEL TOWNSLEY ROGERS
★ ALLAN VAUGHAN
ELSTON
★ GARNETT
RADCLIFFE

160 Pages
All Stories Complete

35

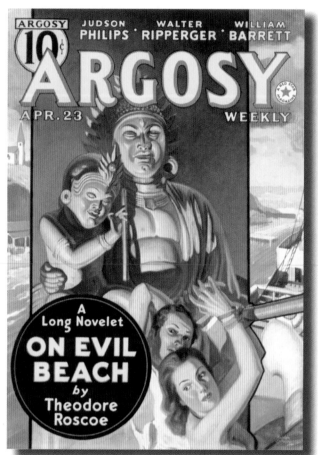

ARGOSY
JUDSON **PHILIPS** · WALTER **RIPPERGER** · WILLIAM **BARRETT**
10¢
ARGOSY
APR. 23
WEEKLY

A
Long Novelet
**ON EVIL
BEACH**
by
Theodore
Roscoe

36

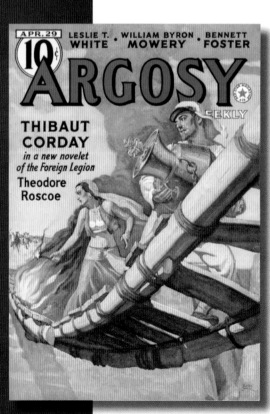

APR. 29
LESLIE T. **WHITE** · WILLIAM BYRON **MOWERY** · BENNETT **FOSTER**
10¢
ARGOSY
WEEKLY

**THIBAUT
CORDAY**
*in a new novelet
of the Foreign Legion*
Theodore
Roscoe

37

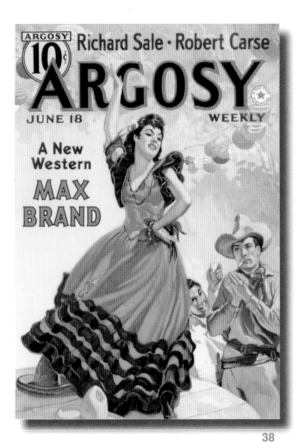

38

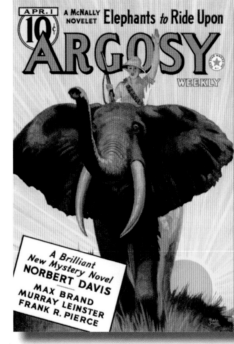

39

40

41

FROM THE SKYSCRAPERS TO JUNGLE VINES

Image 42
ARGOSY
NOVEMBER 13 1937
L. Ron Hubbard, normally a science fiction author, wrote adventure stories for ARGOSY.

Image 43
ARGOSY
MAY 20 1939

Image 44
ARGOSY
AUGUST 20 1938

Image 45
ARGOSY
FEBRUARY 19 1938
Keystone Cops?

Image 46
ARGOSY
SEPTEMBER 24 1938
When All-American Fiction was cancelled, it was folded into ARGOSY.

Image 47
ARGOSY
AUGUST 5 1939
Ancient evil, a story combination of science fiction and horror.

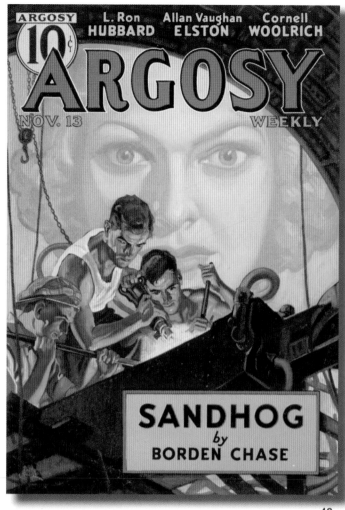

42

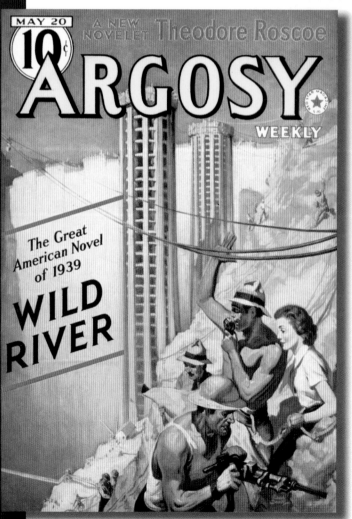

43

ARGOSY 10¢

A NEW NOVEL **Donald Barr Chidsey**

AUG. 20 WEEKLY

KING MIDAS OF THE MOUNTAINS

44

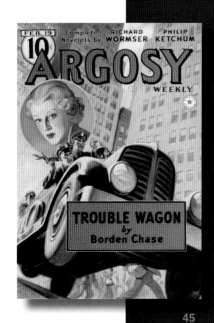

ARGOSY FEB. 19 10¢

Complete Novelets by **RICHARD WORMSER** · **PHILIP KETCHUM**

WEEKLY

TROUBLE WAGON by **Borden Chase**

45

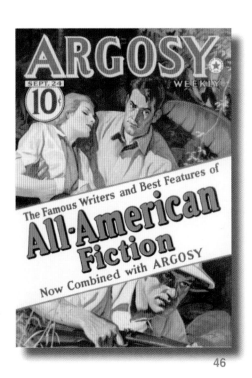

ARGOSY SEPT. 24 10¢ WEEKLY

The Famous Writers and Best Features of

All-American Fiction

Now Combined with ARGOSY

46

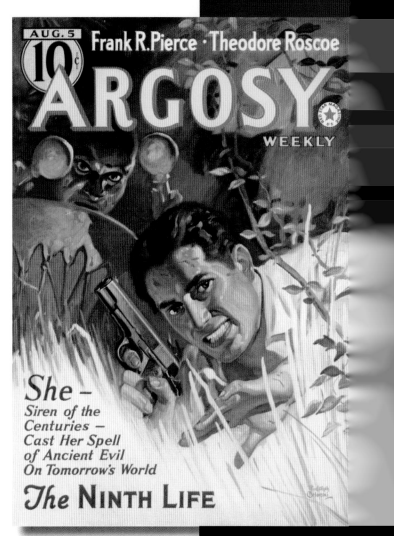

ARGOSY AUG. 5 10¢

Frank R. Pierce · Theodore Roscoe

WEEKLY

She – Siren of the Centuries – Cast Her Spell of Ancient Evil On Tomorrow's World

The NINTH LIFE

47

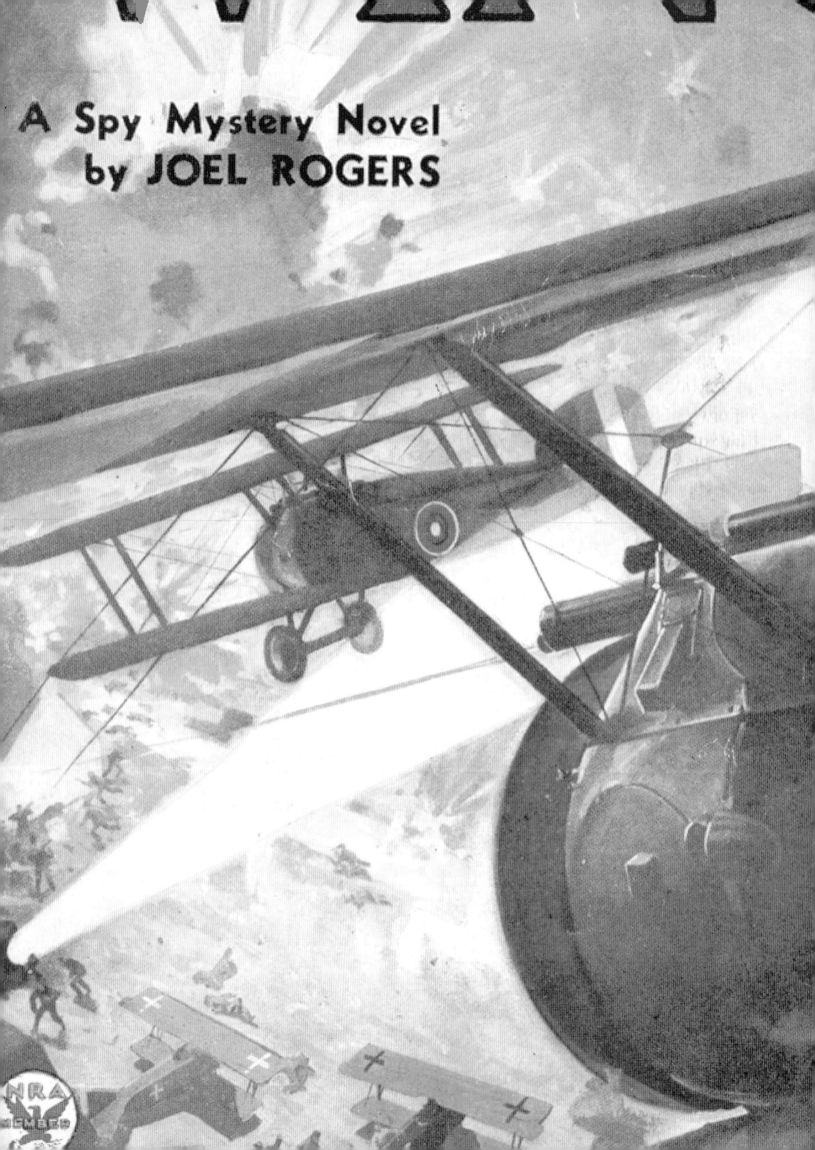

A Spy Mystery Novel
by JOEL ROGERS

"DEATH TRIPS
THE GUNS"

An ace novel by
a new writer

THOMAS
CARPENTER

20c

SPANDAUS AND SPADS

⭐ ⭐ ⭐ ⭐ ⭐

DURING THE late 20's, pulp publishers tried out many specialized titles, magazines with fiction that appealed to a central theme. Gangsters, Fire Fighters, Spies, Navy Stories and, inspired by the real-life miracle of flight, the aviation magazines. **AIR STORIES** from Fiction House was the first aviation title, but it was soon followed by a host of others, including Dell's **WAR BIRDS**. Belarski's talented brush produced art for nearly all of them.

Nearly a decade after World War I ended, and another decade prior to World War II, aviation pulps had stories about barnstorming, flying circuses, postal carriers by aircraft and of course those daring flying knights of World War I. Aviators from the Great War were romanticized well before the pulpwood editors got their hooks into them. Flying machines made of canvas and wood, exceeding speeds of 60 mph, looping and rolling without parachute or fear, World War I aviators made the perfect subject for countless covers.

Instead of depicting dogfights from afar, Belarski got us in tight with the action. Tightly-cropped faces staring through their gun sights. Searchlight-blinded pilots making a strafing run on a German airfield. Wounded defiant pilots cursing an unseen enemy as he goes down in flames.

Pulp magazines started to make the change from World War I stories to more modern yarns just prior to America becoming embroiled in the conflict. Without American boys officially in the war, Ned Pines started **RAF ACES**, highlighting Canadian and British RAF pilots' desperate battle against the Nazi Luftwaffe. This magazine didn't last too long as Pearl Harbor changed everything.

1

2

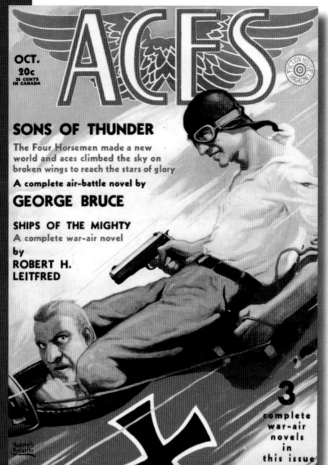

3

4

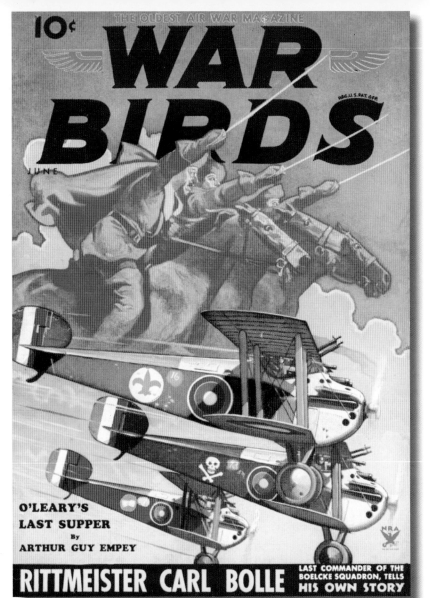

THE OLDEST AIR WAR MAGAZINE

10¢

WAR BIRDS

JUNE

REG. U.S. PAT. OFF.

O'LEARY'S
LAST SUPPER
By
ARTHUR GUY EMPEY

RITTMEISTER CARL BOLLE

LAST COMMANDER OF THE
BOELCKE SQUADRON, TELLS
HIS OWN STORY

5

THE BIGGEST SKY MAGAZINE

AIRPLANE STORIES

ILLUSTRATED   160 PAGE WING SPREAD

April
25¢
30¢ IN CANADA

The Sky of Crumpled Men
A COMPLETE NOVEL
by A.L.H. Bucklin

Other Stories by
John Gerard
Geoffrey Harwood
Edward Price Ehrich
Gil Brewer
Jefferson A. Dewar
Ace Williams
C.L. Edholm

6

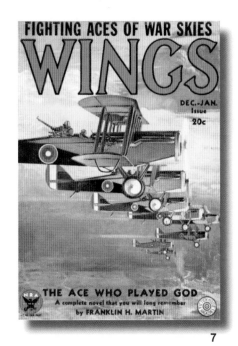

FIGHTING ACES OF WAR SKIES

WINGS

DEC.-JAN.
Issue
20¢

THE ACE WHO PLAYED GOD
A complete novel that you will long remember
by FRANKLIN H. MARTIN

7

FIGHTING ACES OF WAR SKIES

WINGS

JULY
20¢

FRANKLIN
H. MARTIN'S

mighty new novel—
the war-prayer of
ten million valiant
fighting men—

8

"Gott mit uns!"

The First Air Story Magazine!

AiR STORIES

THE SKY-JACKER

Freebooters fly uncharted
skies on the trail of treasure loot.

Complete air-adventure novel by
HERMAN PETERSEN

Air action stories by
**CURTIS MITCHELL
F. N. LITTEN**

SEPT.
20c
25 CENTS
IN CANADA

9

The magazine of AIR-ADVENTURE STORIES

WINGS

April
20c
25 CENTS
IN CANADA

A New Ace
Air-Circus
Novelet by
GEORGE BRUCE

LEVIATHAN OF THE SKY

A Complete Novel of Modern
Air Adventure by
THEODORE A. TINSLEY

10

ACES

DEC.
20c
25 CENTS
IN CANADA

3
Complete
war-air
novels
in this issue

THE LAUGHING MAJOR

A new complete war novel of the air aces
by **GEORGE BRUCE**

11

12

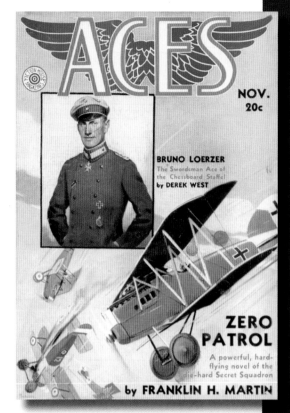

13

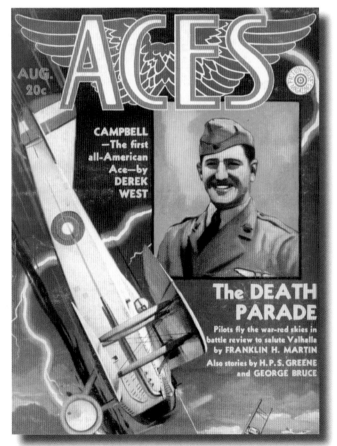

14

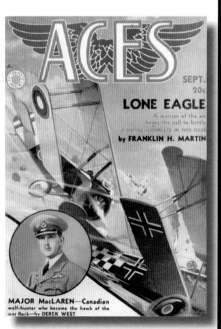

15

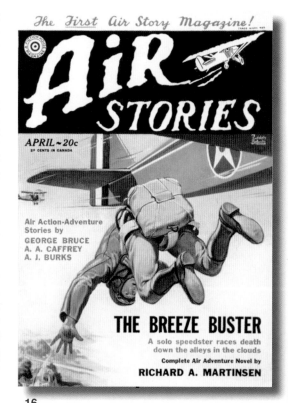

16

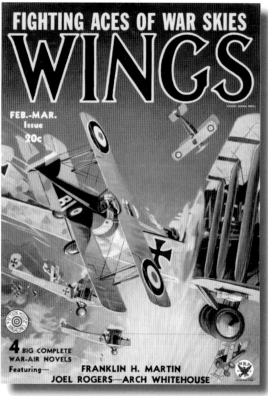

17

18

19

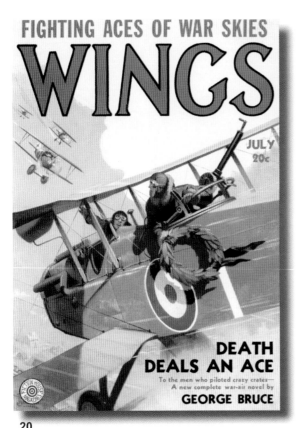

FIGHTING ACES OF WAR SKIES
WINGS

JULY
20c

**DEATH
DEALS AN ACE**

To the men who piloted crazy crates—
A new complete war-air novel by
GEORGE BRUCE

20

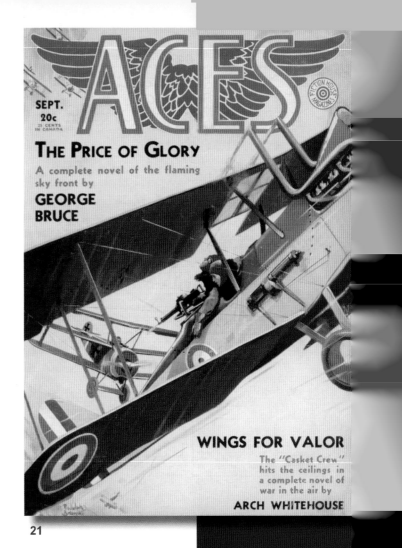

ACES

SEPT.
20c
25 CENTS
IN CANADA

THE PRICE OF GLORY
A complete novel of the flaming
sky front by
**GEORGE
BRUCE**

WINGS FOR VALOR
The "Casket Crew"
hits the ceilings in
a complete novel of
war in the air by
ARCH WHITEHOUSE

21

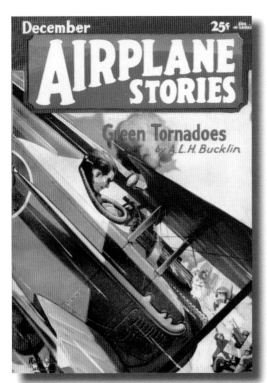

December
25f
30c IN CANADA

AIRPLANE
STORIES

Green Tornadoes
by A.L.H. Bucklin

22

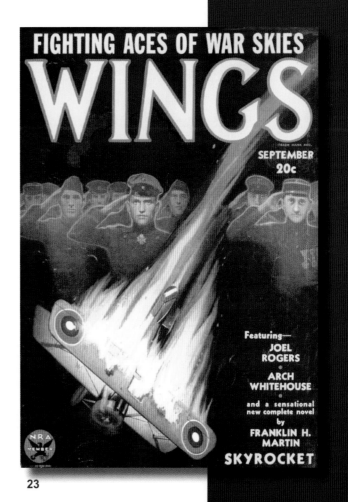

FIGHTING ACES OF WAR SKIES
WINGS

SEPTEMBER
20c

TRADE MARK REG.

Featuring—
**JOEL
ROGERS**

**ARCH
WHITEHOUSE**

and a sensational
new complete novel
by
**FRANKLIN H.
MARTIN**

SKYROCKET

23

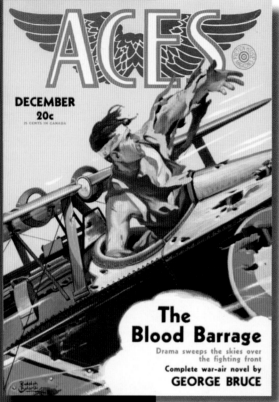

ACES

DECEMBER
20c
25 CENTS IN CANADA

The Blood Barrage

Drama sweeps the skies over
the fighting front

Complete war-air novel by
GEORGE BRUCE

24

FIGHTING ACES OF WAR SKIES

WINGS

January
20c

THE ZERO FLIGHT

They jumped off into
a sky that rained Fokkers
and Spandau steel
A complete war-air novel

by **GEORGE BRUCE**

25

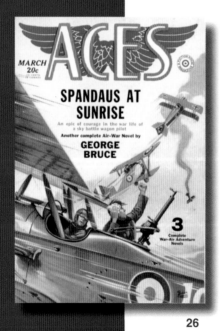

ACES

MARCH
20c

SPANDAUS AT SUNRISE

An epic of courage in the war life of
a sky battle wagon pilot

Another complete Air-War Novel by
GEORGE BRUCE

3
Complete
War-Air Adventure
Novels

26

FIGHTING ACES OF WAR SKIES

WINGS

SEPT.
20c

HELL'S HELMSMAN

The terror of the skies swept
through the night—and a Yank
led the Hun raider-fleet...

A cloud-cracking novel of red-hot
guns in the cold gray skies

COMPLETE IN THIS ISSUE

by **ARCH WHITEHOUSE**

28

FIGHTING ACES OF WAR SKIES

WINGS

OCTOBER
20c

"THE BIG 3"

JOEL ROGERS
FRANKLIN H. MARTIN
ARCH. WHITEHOUSE

27

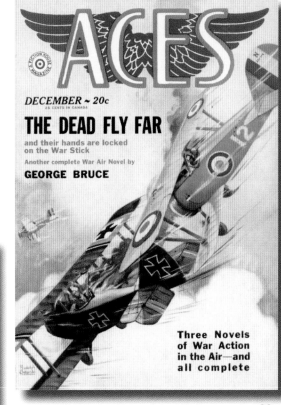

30

29

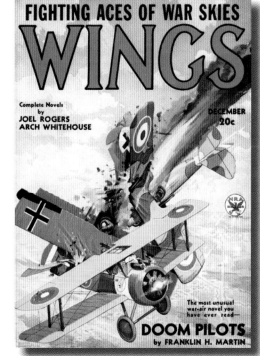

32

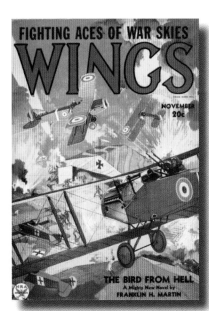

31

**Image 33
WINGS
DECEMBER 1932**
Another harassed Allied
bomber.

**Image 34
WINGS
FEBRUARY 1935**
Coming to the cross-
roads. One of the last
issues published monthly.
WINGS is about to go
quarterly like a good number of other Fiction House
titles.

**Image 35
WINGS
AUGUST 1931**
Frederick Davis was bet-
ter known as a detective
yarn author. He also
originated the detective
hero character The Moon
Man.

**Image 36
WINGS
FEBRUARY 1932**
An Allied Spy is rescued.

**Image 37
WINGS
OCTOBER 1932**
One of the last issues
prior to Fiction House
shutting down all of their
publication's due to one of
the publishers death.

**Image 38
WINGS
SPRING 1938**
One of the last covers
Rudolph Belarski painted
for WINGS.

33

34

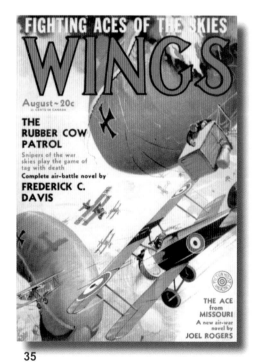

35

36

37

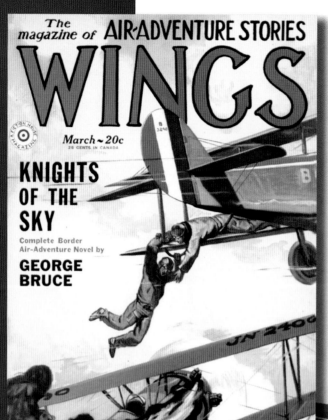

The magazine of **AIR-ADVENTURE STORIES**
WINGS

MARCH ~ 20c
25 CENTS IN CANADA

KNIGHTS OF THE SKY

Complete Border
Air-Adventure Novel by
GEORGE BRUCE

39

ACES

SEPT.
20c
25 CENTS
IN CANADA

The SPY SQUAD

An epic novel
of the air-war front
by **JOEL ROGERS**

40

34

41

42

44

43

45

46

FIGHTING DAREDEVILS OF TODAY'S WAR

AIR WAR

10¢

WINTER ISSUE

CAPTAIN DANGER'S CHALLENGE

An Exciting Novelet By LT. SCOTT MORGAN

BUY WAR BONDS AND STAMPS FOR VICTORY!

TARNISHED WINGS
A Novelet of Fighting Aces By ANGUS FULLER

A THRILLING PUBLICATION

47

10¢

True Action Stories of the Men With Wings

RAF ACES

WINTER ISSUE

BRITISH WINGS
A Complete Book-Length Sky Action Novel By ROBERT SIDNEY BOWEN

DEATH WRITES THE ORDERS
A Complete Novelet By ALFRED H. IBBOTSON

A THRILLING PUBLICATION

48

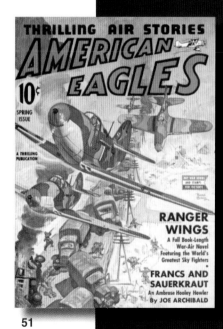

THRILLING AIR STORIES

AMERICAN EAGLES

10¢ SPRING ISSUE

A THRILLING PUBLICATION

BUY WAR BONDS AND STAMPS FOR VICTORY

RANGER WINGS
A Full Book-Length War-Air Novel Featuring the World's Greatest Sky Fighters

FRANCS AND SAUERKRAUT
An Ambrose Hooley Howler By JOE ARCHIBALD

51

ARMY ★ NAVY

FLYING STORIES

10¢

First Issue

A THRILLING PUBLICATION

FLYING FOR MacARTHUR
A Novel of War in the Philippines By LAURENCE DONOVAN

THE CALL TO YOUTH
By MAJOR GENERAL BARTON K. YOUNT
Commanding General, Air Corps Flying Training Command

50

10¢ NOV.

A THRILLING PUBLICATION

SKY FIGHTERS

Ace of the **RED STAR**
An Exciting Action Novel By JOE ARCHIBALD

BUY WAR BONDS AND STAMPS FOR VICTORY

CHINESE MISSION
A Complete Novelet By NORMAN A. DANIELS

49

52

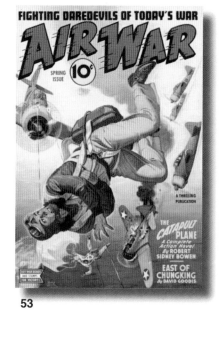

53

54

55

56

57

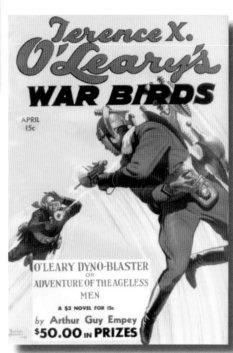

58

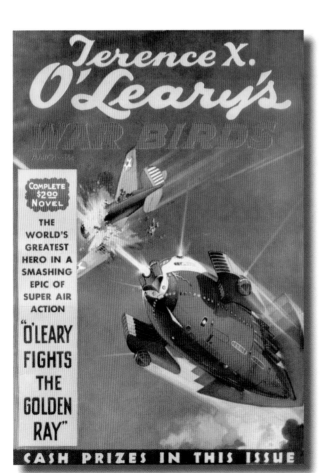

59

DETECTI

THE GLITTERING COFFINS

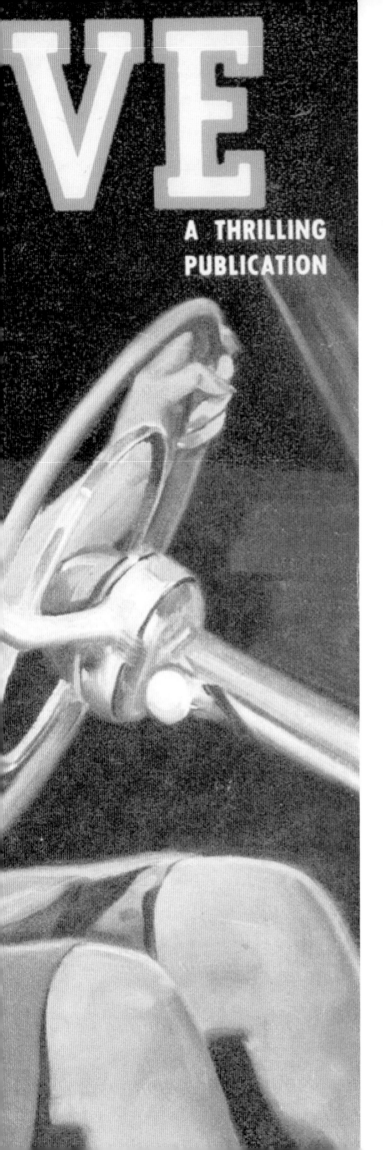

GATS, GAMS AND GUMSHOES

DETECTIVE PULPS were a mainstay of the industry. The number of murders that filled the pages monthly of all the titles would have packed the morgues in every big city in America. Pulp readers couldn't get enough of mystery and mayhem and the number of detective titles found monthly on newsstands dwarfing almost all other genres outside of the Western magazines.

From the publishing offices of Frank Munsey and Ned Pines, Rudy Belarski was in demand and had a continuous market for cover art. For Munsey he painted covers for **DOUBLE DETECTIVE** and **DETECTIVE FICTION WEEKLY**. For Pines' Standard Publications/Thrilling Group he decorated the covers for a myriad of magazines with **THRILLING DETECTIVE**, **G-MEN** and **POPULAR DETECTIVE** receiving the bulk of his hard work.

Belarski filled his detective canvases with action seemingly an instant away from mayhem, and that moment just after. A scream captured just prior to it being heard. A gunshot frozen a scant microsecond before the bullet hits its target, or a body yet to fall, mortally wounded from the dagger protruding from the back. The male thugs that Belarski painted threatened with a trunk full of weapons at their disposal. They included the famous Thompson submachine gun, a favorite of the 20's and 30's gangsters; the infamous German Luger; knives, bare knuckles and those often-portrayed but deadly .45 automatics. One of the male models repeated by Belarski appears to have been Edward Magner, who also posed for George Rozen as the famous hawk-nosed countenance of The Shadow.

Not only were the men deadly, but the women as well. Belarski became known for his alluring women, both those in peril and the femme fatale creating danger. His women were rarely in repose unless trussed, perhaps gagged and/or dead. Outside of having more clothes, Belarski's women would have been—ah—well comfortable on the covers of another pulp title fondly remembered today, **SPICY DETECTIVE**.

One problem that Belarski was faced with in creating covers for detective magazines was his need for models. Planes and battle scenes were one thing, but alluringly-figured women bound and gagged was another. While residing in New York City, professional models were easily accessible. After moving to New Rochelle, NY bringing models out to his home studio in the suburbs was difficult and expensive. Much the same as Norman Saunders, Belarski began using a photography studio to shoot images for his reference material. This later proved to be a much welcomed necessity.

Belarski filled the covers for countless detective pulps for nearly fifteen years, with many of his assignments coming from Churchill Ettinger, one of the art directors for Ned Pines' Thrilling line of publications. As the pulps died out from under them, Pines' Standard Publications entered the paperback field under their imprint Popular Library. Brought along on this endeavor was art directors Churchill Ettinger who turn brought his favorite artist Belarski into the paperback field.

1

2

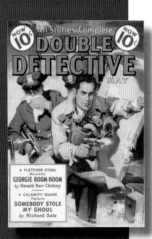

3

4

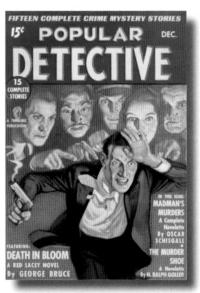

5

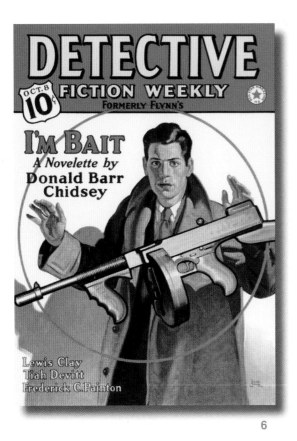

6

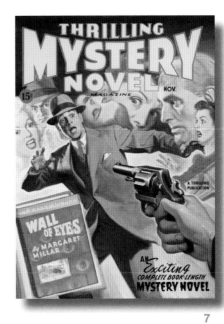

7

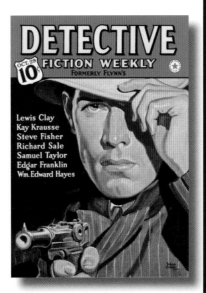

8

9

BABES IN BONDAGE!

Image 10
5 DETECTIVE
NOVELS MAGAZINE
FALL 1950

Image 11
MYSTERY BOOK
MAGAZINE
SUMMER 1948
Brett Halliday's character
Mike Shayne prior to his own
digest publication.

Image 12
POPULAR DETECTIVE
MARCH 1950
Race Williams spanned a
number of pulp titles, from
BLACK MASK through DIME
DETECTIVE MAGAZINE.

Image 13
G-MEN DETECTIVE
MARCH 1949
Robert Sidney Bowen was
one of the many authors
who penned the Dan Fowler
character that was featured
in G-MEN DETECTIVE.

Image 14
THRILLING DETECTIVE
JUNE 1948
Robert Leslie Bellem was
better known for his charac-
ter Dan Turner, Hollywood
Detective.

Image 15
DETECTIVE FICTION
WEEKLY
FEBRUARY 18 1939
Satanism wasn't a widely
used cover theme.

Image 16
GIANT DETECTIVE
WINTER 1951
GIANT DETECTIVE was one
of the last pulp magazines,
prior to the publisher turning
to paperback books full time.

Image 17
DOUBLE DETECTIVE
JUNE 1939
Richard Sale went from a
pulp magazine wordsmith
to screenplay writer in
Hollywood.

10

11

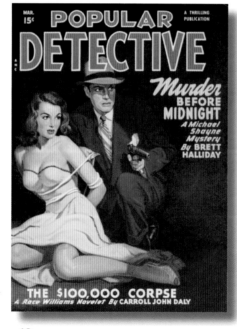

12

13

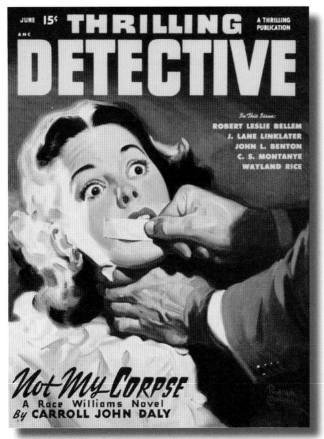

JUNE 15¢ A THRILLING PUBLICATION

THRILLING
DETECTIVE

In This Issue:
ROBERT LESLIE BELLEM
J. LANE LINKLATER
JOHN L. BENTON
C. S. MONTANYE
WAYLAND RICE

Not My Corpse
A Race Williams Novel
By CARROLL JOHN DALY

14

DETECTIVE
FICTION WEEKLY
FEB. 18 10¢ FORMERLY FLYNN'S

The BLACK
MAGIC
MURDERS
A Short Novel by
DALE CLARK

15

THE BEST IN NEW
MYSTERY FICTION

Detective

WINTER 25¢

THE DEEP,
DARK GRAVE
a novelet of suspense
By BRUNO FISCHER

A THRILLING
PUBLICATION

FEATURING
**THE BLONDE
BROUGHT BULLETS**
an exciting full-length mystery novel
By GENE RIDER

16

All Stories Complete

NOW 10¢ **NOW 10¢**

DOUBLE
DETECTIVE
JUNE

An Eerie Novelette
John Lawrence

A Calamity Quade
Feature
Richard Sale

Donald Barr Chidsey
Edwin Truett
Dale Clark
and others

17

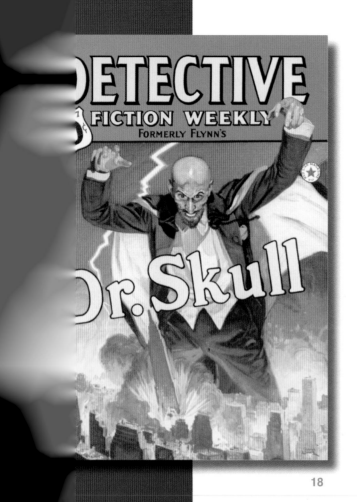

DETECTIVE
FICTION WEEKLY
FORMERLY FLYNN'S

Dr. Skull

18

DETECTIVE
FICTION WEEKLY
FORMERLY FLYNN'S
OCT. 2 10¢

A
Daffy Dill
Novelette
by
RICHARD
SALE

19

DETECTIVE
FICTION WEEKLY
FORMERLY FLYNN'S
JAN. 14 10¢

3 COMPLETE NOVELETTES

Hugh B. Cave
Paul Ernst
T. T. Flynn

CYPHER SECRETS

True Crime Features

International Spies and Political Racketeers Meet Death at a
Midnight Deadline

20

10 Stories - All Complete!
DETECTIVE
FICTION WEEKLY
SEPT. 11 10¢

Dancing Death
A Complete Short Novel by
Eric Taylor

21

22

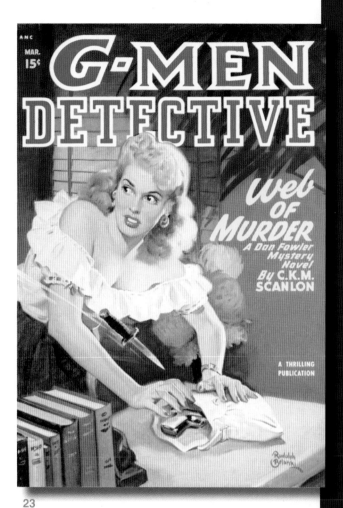

23

24

26

25

A PICTURE PERFECT CRIME

Image 27
THRILLING DETECTIVE
APRIL 1947

Image 28
THRILLING DETECTIVE
AUGUST 1948
Nick Ransom featured is a direct brother of Dan Turner.

Image 29
THRILLING DETECTIVE
JANUARY 1944

Image 30
DETECTIVE FICTION
WEEKLY
APRIL 8 1939

Image 31
DOUBLE DETECTIVE
AUGUST 1938
Woolrich wrote a short story that later became "Rear Window" in DIME DETECTIVE MAGAZINE.

STOP CLOWNING AROUND!

Image 32
DETECTIVE NOVELS
MAGAZINE
FEBRUARY 1944
Candid Camera Kid was actually written by Norman Daniels.

Image 33
POPULAR DETECTIVE
JUNE 1945

Image 34
DETECTIVE FICTION
WEEKLY
MAY 21 1938

Image 35
MYSTERY BOOK
MAGAZINE
SPRING 1948
Fredric Brown is considered one the best all-around pulp authors who ever graced a page.

Image 36
DETECTIVE FICTION
WEEKLY
DECEMBER 3 1938

27

28

29

30

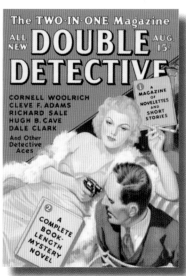

31

32

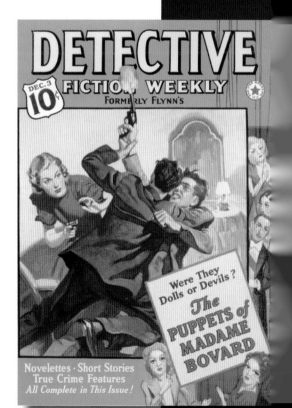

33

34

35

36

THE FEDERALS IN ACTION

10¢

G-MEN

JAN.

A THRILLING PUBLICATION

TONG WAR!
Featuring the World's Greatest Man Hunters in a Complete Full-length Novel

THE BOMB SYNDICATE
By FRANKIE LEWIS

37

FIFTEEN COMPLETE CRIME MYSTERY STORIES

15¢

POPULAR

NOV.

DETECTIVE

15 COMPLETE STORIES

A THRILLING PUBLICATION

DEATH ORCHIDS
A Complete Novel
By MAXWELL HAWKINS

GRANDMA from HELL
By MARGIE HARRIS

HANGMAN'S ROPE
By THEODORE TINSLEY

AND
12 OTHER
GRIPPING
MYSTERIES
By
POPULAR
AUTHORS

38

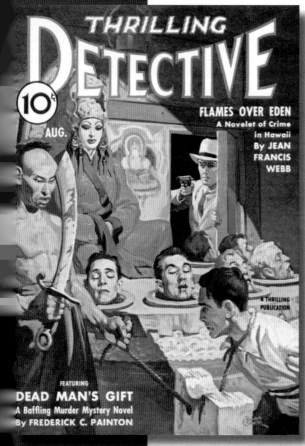

THRILLING

DETECTIVE

10¢

AUG.

FLAMES OVER EDEN
A Novelet of Crime in Hawaii
By JEAN FRANCIS WEBB

A THRILLING PUBLICATION

FEATURING
DEAD MAN'S GIFT
A Baffling Murder Mystery Novel
By FREDERICK C. PAINTON

39

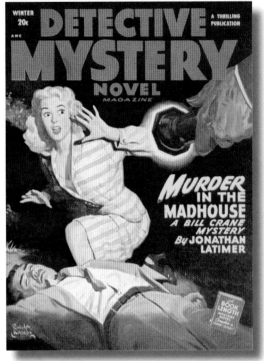

40

41

42

43

44

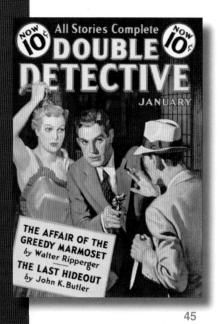

45

46

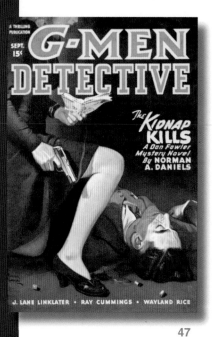

47

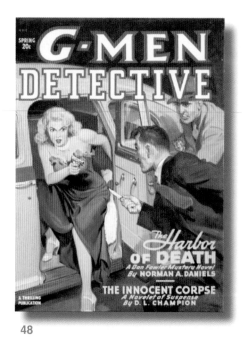

48

49

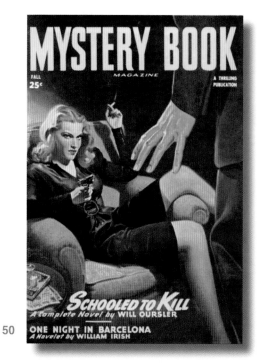

50

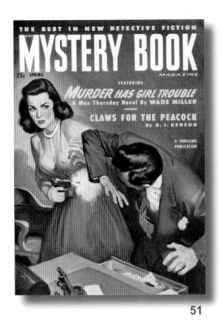

THE BEST IN NEW DETECTIVE FICTION

MYSTERY BOOK
MAGAZINE

25¢ SPRING

FEATURING

MURDER HAS GIRL TROUBLE
A Max Thursday Novel By WADE MILLER

CLAWS FOR THE PEACOCK
By B. J. BENSON

A THRILLING PUBLICATION

51

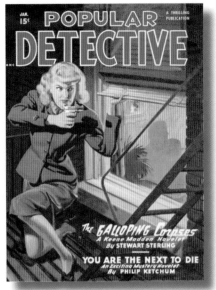

JAN.
15¢

POPULAR DETECTIVE
AND

A THRILLING PUBLICATION

The GALLOPING Corpses
A Keene Madden Novelet
By STEWART STERLING

YOU ARE THE NEXT TO DIE
An Exciting Mystery Novelet
By PHILIP KETCHUM

52

FIFTEEN COMPLETE CRIME MYSTERY STORIES

15¢
FEB.

POPULAR DETECTIVE

15 COMPLETE STORIES

A THRILLING PUBLICATION

15 COMPLETE STORIES

MURDER TO ORDER
A Complete Novel
By RICHARD B. SALE

DEATH BY INCHES
A G-Man Novelette
By ARTHUR J. BURKS

MYSTERY OF THE VAMPIRE BAT
A Complete Novelette
By PRESTON GRADY

53

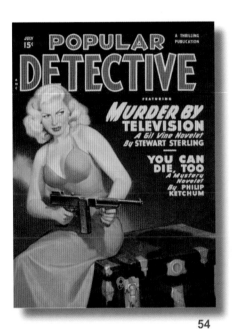

JULY
15¢

POPULAR DETECTIVE
AND

A THRILLING PUBLICATION

FEATURING

MURDER BY TELEVISION
A Gil Vine Novelet
By STEWART STERLING

YOU CAN DIE, TOO
A Mystery Novelet
By PHILIP KETCHUM

54

THRILLING DETECTIVE

JAN.
10¢

DEATH IN THE WIND
An Exciting Novelet
By CURTISS

THE SECOND ACT IS MURDER
A Complete Mystery Novelet
By W. T. BALLARD

DOWN TO DANGER
A Baffling Novelet
By J. LANE LINKLATER

55

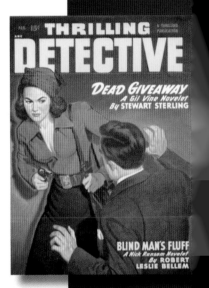

FEB. 15¢

THRILLING DETECTIVE
AND

A THRILLING PUBLICATION

DEAD GIVEAWAY
A Gil Vine Novelet
By STEWART STERLING

BLIND MAN'S FLUFF
A Nick Ransom Novelet
By ROBERT LESLIE BELLEM

56

THRILLING DETECTIVE

15¢ JUNE

THIS CORPSE ON ME
A Race Williams Novel
By CARROLL JOHN DALY

A THRILLING PUBLICATION

KILLING TAKES CONFIDENCE
An Exciting Novelet
By CURTISS T. GARDNER

THE EGG IN THE BIER
A Crime Novelet
By A. J. COLLINS

57

THRILLING DETECTIVE

10¢ SEPT.

SIXTEEN POUNDS OF MURDER
A Baffling Mystery Novelet
By CARL G. HODGES

A THRILLING PUBLICATION

MEET THE KILLER
An Exciting Novelet
By JOHN L. BENTON

THE TRIANGULAR BLADE
A Crime Novelet
By CARTER SPRAGUE

58

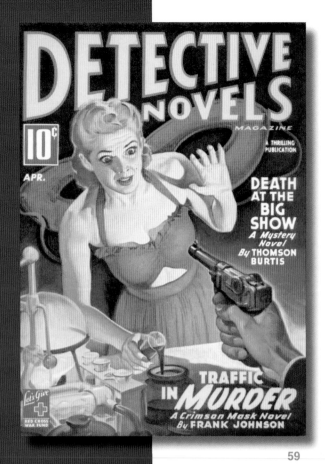

DETECTIVE NOVELS MAGAZINE

10¢

APR.

DEATH AT THE BIG SHOW
A Mystery Novel!
By THOMSON BURTIS

TRAFFIC IN MURDER
A Crimson Mask Novel
By FRANK JOHNSON

Let's Give RED CROSS WAR FUND

59

APR. 15¢ THRILLING
ANC
DETECTIVE
A THRILLING PUBLICATION

In This Issue
HOMICIDE SHAFT
A Nick Ransom Novelet
By ROBERT LESLIE BELLEM

Featuring
NIGHT WITHOUT END
A Mystery Novelet
By WYATT BLASSINGAME

60

OCT. 15¢ THRILLING
ANC
DETECTIVE
A THRILLING PUBLICATION

Hibiscus AND HOMICIDE
A Mystery Novel
By WILLIAM CAMPBELL GAULT

C. S. MONTANYE • JACK KOFOED
WYATT BLASSINGAME • CARL G. HODGES

61

THRILLING MYSTERY NOVEL MAGAZINE MAR.

15¢

A Complete
BOOK-LENGTH MYSTERY NOVEL

The THIRTY-FIRST Bullfinch By HELEN REILLY

A THRILLING PUBLICATION

62

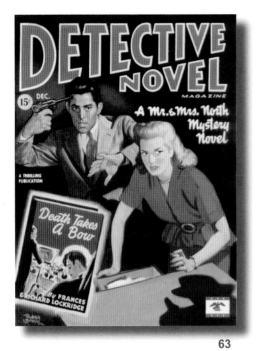

63

64

65

66

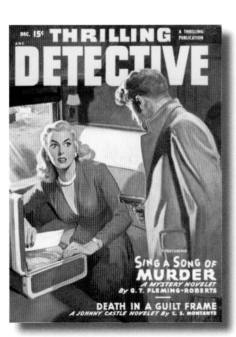

67

68

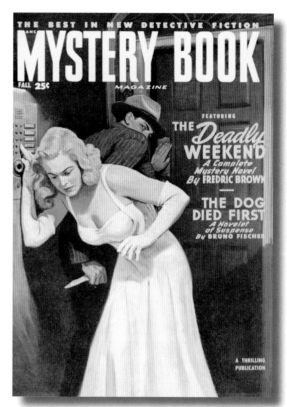

69

70

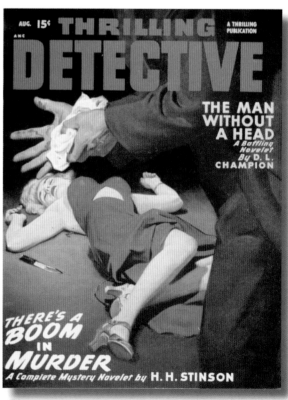

71

72

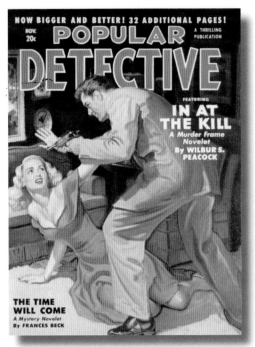

NOW BIGGER AND BETTER! 32 ADDITIONAL PAGES!

NOV. 20¢

A THRILLING PUBLICATION

POPULAR DETECTIVE

FEATURING

IN AT THE KILL

A Murder Frame Novelet

BY WILBUR S. PEACOCK

THE TIME WILL COME

A Mystery Novelet
By FRANCES BECK

73

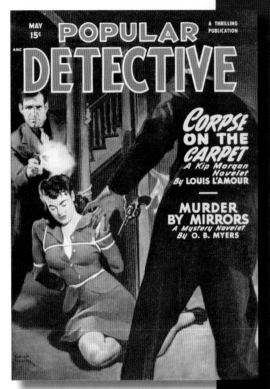

MAY 15¢

A THRILLING PUBLICATION

POPULAR DETECTIVE

CORPSE ON THE CARPET

A Kip Morgan Novelet
By LOUIS L'AMOUR

MURDER BY MIRRORS

A Mystery Novelet
By O. B. MYERS

74

THRILLING DETECTIVE

10¢

NOV.

FEATURING

THE GLASS GUILLOTINE

A Complete Novel of Politics and Crime
By STEWART STERLING

MURDER CAMP

A Complete Mystery Novelet
By BENTON BRADEN

75

DEC 15¢

A THRILLING PUBLICATION

THRILLING DETECTIVE

Haunt Me NO MORE

A Mystery Novel
By EDWARD RONNS

SERENADE WITH SLUGS

A Nick Ransom Novelet
By ROBERT LESLIE BELLEM

76

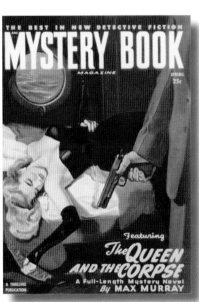

THE BEST IN NEW DETECTIVE FICTION

MYSTERY BOOK

MAGAZINE

SPRING 25¢

Featuring

The QUEEN AND THE CORPSE

A Full-Length Mystery Novel
By MAX MURRAY

A THRILLING PUBLICATION

77

DETECTIVE
FICTION WEEKLY
MAR. 12
10¢
FORMERLY ...

I Wouldn't Be in Your Shoes
by CORNELL WOOLRICH

78

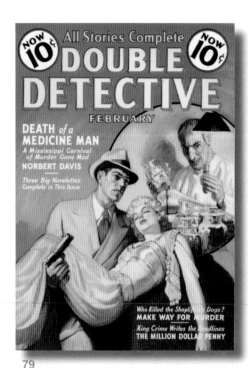

All Stories Complete
NOW 10¢
DOUBLE
DETECTIVE
FEBRUARY
NOW 10¢

DEATH of a
MEDICINE MAN
A Mississippi Carnival of Murder Gone Mad
NORBERT DAVIS
Three Big Novelettes
Complete in This Issue

Who Killed the Shoplifter's Dogs?
MAKE WAY FOR MURDER
King Crime Writes the Headlines
THE MILLION DOLLAR PENNY

79

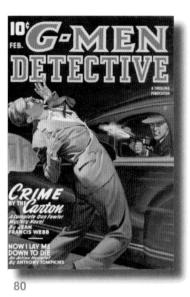

10¢
FEB.
G-MEN
DETECTIVE
A THRILLING
PUBLICATION

Crime
BY THE
Carton
A Complete Dan Fowler
Mystery Novel
By JEAN
FRANCIS WEBB

NOW I LAY ME
DOWN TO DIE
An Action Novelet
By ANTHONY TOMPKINS

80

GIANT
THE BEST IN NEW
MYSTERY FICTION
Detective
FALL
25¢

FEATURING
SIX MINUTES
OF MURDER
A Complete
Book-Length Novel
By WALT SHELDON

DEATH IN ALASKA
A Novelet of an Arctic Manhunt
By WILLIAM DEGENHARD

81

196 PAGES OF NEW DETECTIVE FICTION
MYSTERY BOOK
FALL
25¢

Run to
DEATH
A Peter Duluth Novel
By PATRICK QUENTIN

DARK EXIT
A Novelet
By HELEN REILLY

A THRILLING
PUBLICATION

84

JAN.
20¢
POPULAR
A THRILLING
PUBLICATION
DETECTIVE

IN THIS ISSUE
THE SMELL
OF FEAR
a Gil Vine
novelet by
STEWART
STERLING

FEATURING
ON BORROWED
CRIME
a novelet of
suspense and mystery by
DONN MULLALLY

83

THRILLING
DETECTIVE
NOV
10¢

THE Man FROM
ALCATRAZ
An Exciting Mystery Novel
By JOHN L. BENTON

MURDER OFF THE RECORD
A Johnny Castle Novelet
By C.S. MONTANYE

82

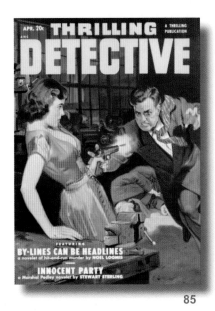

85

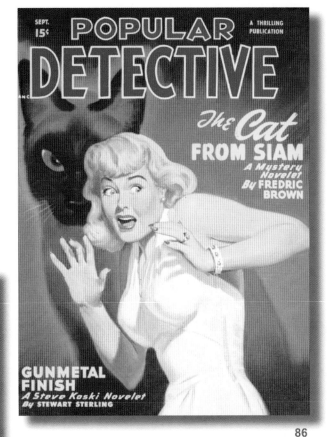

86

87

88

89

90

91

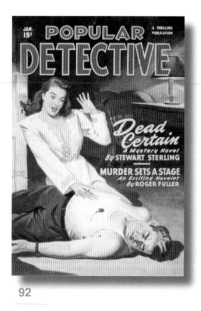

92

93

94

THRILLING DETECTIVE
TOO MANY ARE DEAD
A Complete Mystery Novel
By WILLIAM ROUGH

THE CORPSE WALKED AWAY
An Exciting Novelet
By H. RALPH GOLLER

95

THRILLING DETECTIVE

MAKE MINE MURDER
A Baffling Mystery Novel
By EDWARD RONNS

TOO OLD FOR TROUBLE
By WARD HAWKINS

96

THRILLING DETECTIVE

Don't FORGET YOUR GUN
A Swift-Moving Crime Novel
By WILLIAM CHAMBERLAIN

BLOOD ON HER HANDS
A Mystery Novelet
By TALMAGE POWELL

THE CORPSE FROM RENO
A Blackmail Novelet
By JOHN L. BENTON

97

THRILLING AND DETECTIVE

The Day I DIE
A Complete Mystery Novel
By EDWARD RONNS

PUZZLE IN PERIL
A Rick Ransom Novelet
By ROBERT LESLIE BELLEM

99

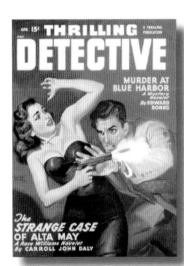

THRILLING DETECTIVE

MURDER AT BLUE HARBOR
A Mystery Novelet
By EDWARD RONNS

The STRANGE CASE OF ALTA MAY
A Race Williams Novelet
By CARROLL JOHN DALY

98

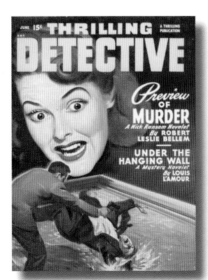

THRILLING AND DETECTIVE

Preview OF MURDER
A Nick Ransom Novelet
By ROBERT LESLIE BELLEM

UNDER THE HANGING WALL
A Mystery Novelet
By LOUIS L'AMOUR

101

THRILLING DETECTIVE

FINGER OF GUILT
By JEAN FRANCIS WEBB

FEATURING
DEATH STALKS BACKSTAGE
A Gripping Complete Novelet
By FRANK JOHNSON

100

102

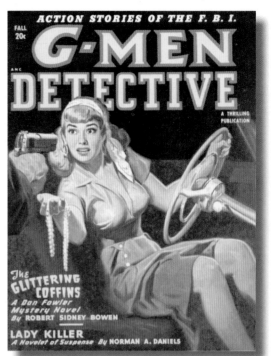

103

104

105

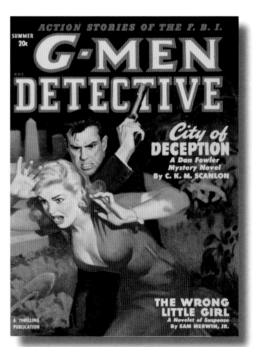

106

107

108

109

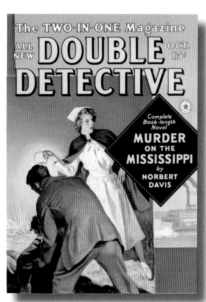

110

111

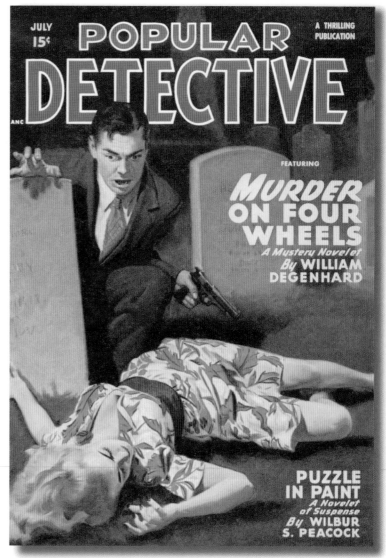

112

Image 112
POPULAR DETECTIVE
JULY 1949
This guy hopefully isn't a tombstone salesman drumming up more business.

Image 113
POPULAR DETECTIVE
SEPTEMBER 1947
Although David Goodis wrote more mysteries for the paperbacks, most of his pulp output was for aviation titles. Here is one of the few times he appeared in a detective magazine.

Image 114
POPULAR DETECTIVE
NOVEMBER 1949
Another cover that was later used on a Popular Library paperback title.

Image 115
MYSTERY BOOK MAGAZINE
SPRING 1949
Travis McGee was MacDonald's most famous character and yet Travis never appeared in pulp form, strictly in paperback and hardback editions.

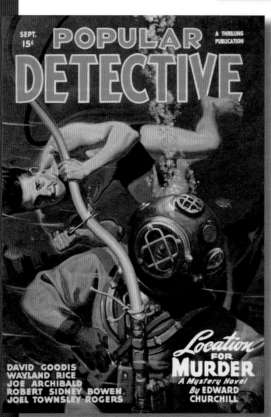

113

NOV.
15¢

POPULAR DETECTIVE

A THRILLING
PUBLICATION

Murder OFF HONDURAS
A Mystery Novelet
By DAVID DODGE

THE DEAD DON'T DIE
A Gripping Novelet By BRUNO FISCHER

114

IN NEW DETECTIVE FICTION

MYSTERY BOOK
MAGAZINE

SPRING
25¢

A THRILLING
PUBLICATION

*Three
Complete Novelets*
*BLACK
REMINDER*
By HELEN REILLY

MURDER
MIRAGE
By WESTMORELAND GRAY

A CORPSE IN
HIS DREAMS
By JOHN D. MacDONALD

115

THRILLING
DETECTIVE

10¢

MAY

Death
ON SKIS
An Exciting Mystery Novel
By EDWARD CHURCHILL

DON'T MEDDLE
WITH MURDER
A Johnny Castle Novelet
By C. S. MONTANYE

A THRILLING
PUBLICATION

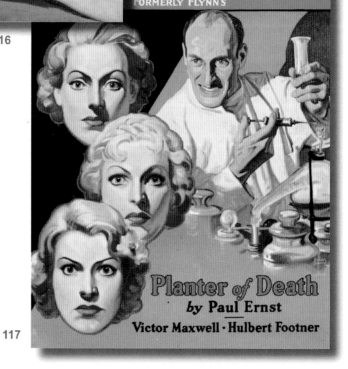

TECTIVE
TION WEEKLY
FORMERLY FLYNN'S

Planter of Death
by Paul Ernst

Victor Maxwell · Hulbert Footner

116

117

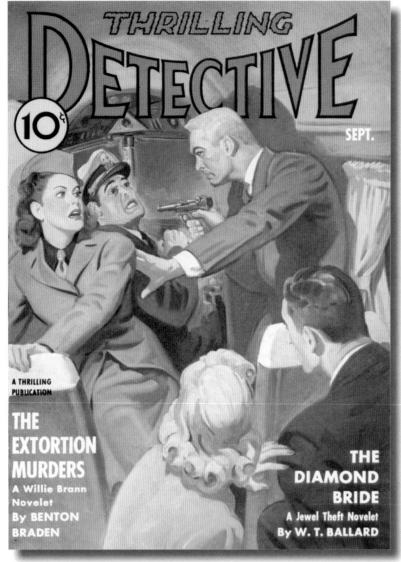

118

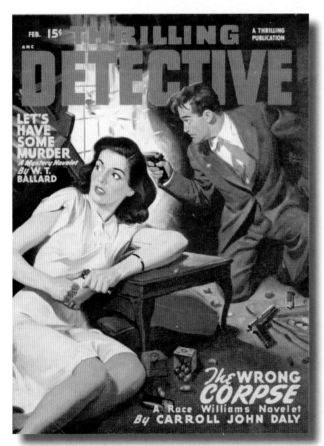

119

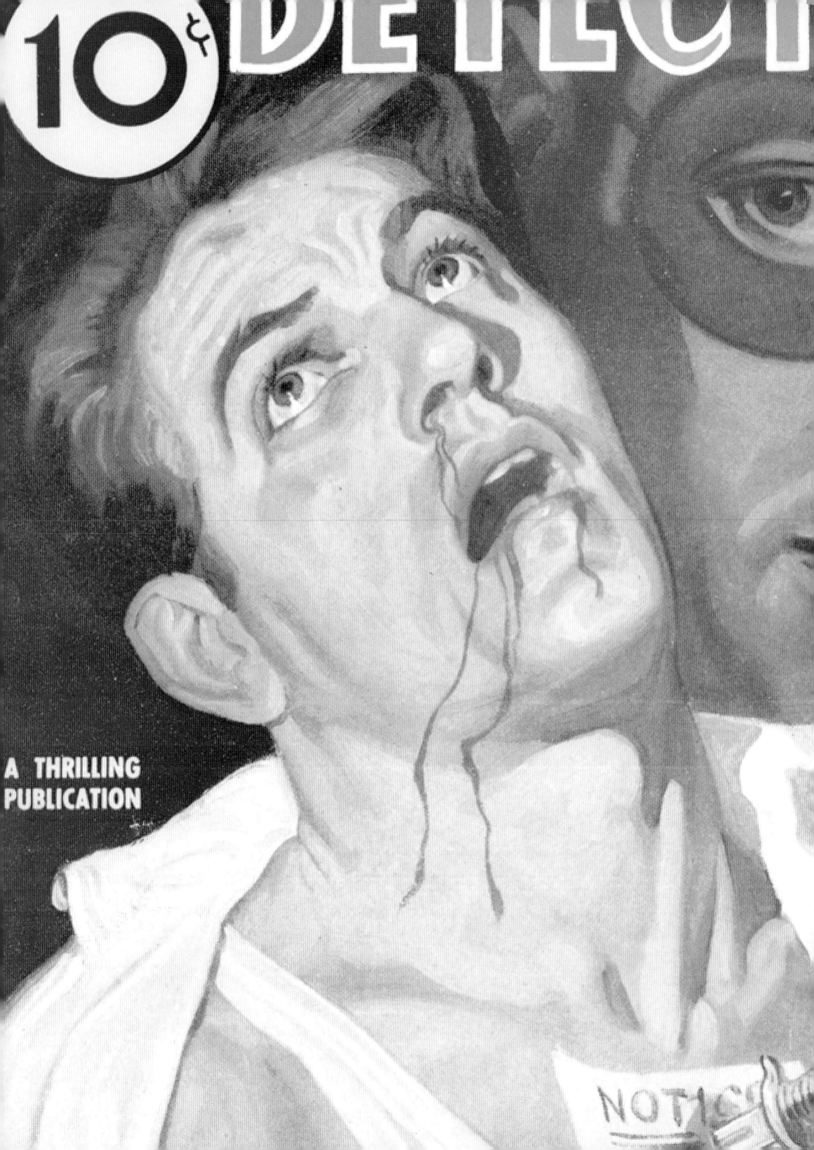

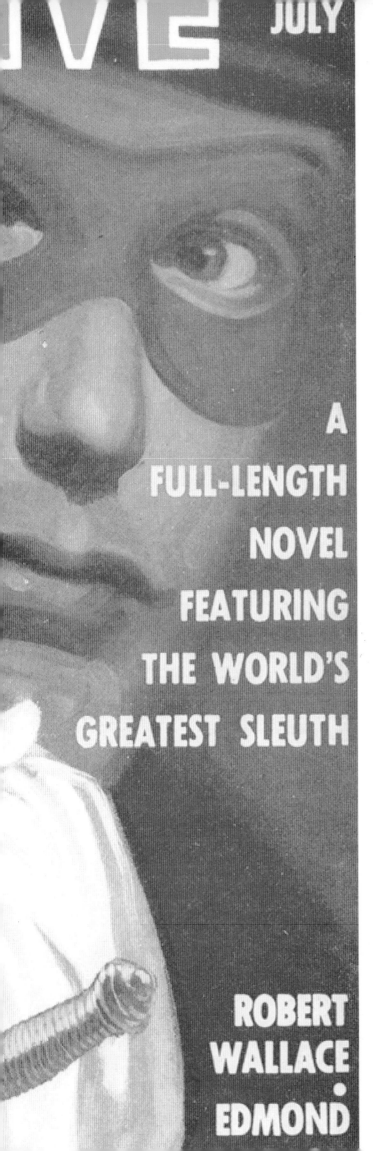

JULY

A
FULL-LENGTH
NOVEL
FEATURING
THE WORLD'S
GREATEST SLEUTH

ROBERT
WALLACE
EDMOND

HEROES AND FLOATING HEADS

THE HERO pulp gene was invented by Street & Smith, publisher of **THE SHADOW MAGAZINE**. Like any other successful genre, pulp publishers jumped on the bandwagon to capitalize on a good idea. Ned Pines and his Thrilling Group were no different. Less than a year after **THE SHADOW** hit the stands, **THE PHANTOM DETECTIVE** took up his cape and unrivaled powers of deduction to battle crime and evil.

It was eight years after first publishing **THE PHANTOM DETECTIVE**, that Pines decided to made a change with his straight-laced pulp, **BLACK BOOK DETECTIVE**. Pines commissioned pulp veteran Norman Daniels to produce a hero whose monthly stories would be featured in **BLACK BOOK DETECTIVE**. Daniels' created Tony Quinn aka The Black Bat that shares an unlikely heritage with DC Comics **BATMAN** character. Through an astounding coincidence both hit newsstands at nearly the same time in 1939, with both based upon a bat-like persona.

What ties these two hero pulp characters together is a decision by the art director at Thrilling to feature the faces of the main characters—masked or cowled as each may be — floating above some action of foul play on the cover. Month after month their visage was seen peering spectrally over the shoulders of evil-doers, offering a glimpse of the retribution to come by issues end.

Issue after issue The Black Bat and The Phantom Detective swung into action, bringing the guilty parties of urban crime to justice. Whereas The Shadow, The Spider or Doc Savage fought against more desperate odds, often saving the entire world from some mass menace, The Black Bat and The Phantom Detective's exploits dealt in more down to earth crime and punishment. Although this was not often immediately apparent from the lurid, action packed covers brought to life by the individual talents of Rudolph Belarski.

While **THE PHANTOM DETECTIVE** and **BLACK BOOK DETECTIVE** proved to be good assignments for an artist by their long-running consistency and the stability of the income they offered, years after he had retired, Belarski once complained to an interviewer that the compositional constraints of these covers were a pain in the ass. Yet his deft hand with design made the best of the soon repetitious theme. A number of the original Black Bat covers were later turned into paperback covers by painting out and removing the floating head of the Black Bat. This reuse of art could only have been done if the foreground action was sufficient, and in Belarski's case quite obviously it was, and murder and mayhem once again was targeted on innocent victims in the new paperback format.

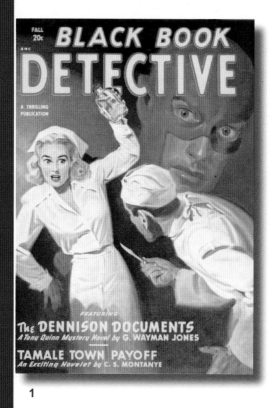

1

2

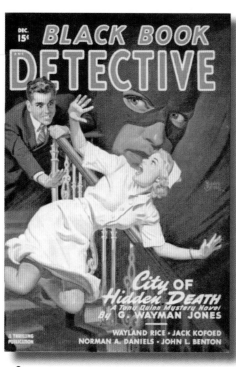

3

BLACK BOOK
DETECTIVE

JAN.
20¢

THIRTY-ONE
DEADLY GUNS
A Tony Quinn Mystery Novel
By G. WAYMAN JONES

THUNDER IN
STONY FLATS
An Action Novelet
By A. J. COLLINS

A THRILLING
PUBLICATION

5

The PHANTOM
DETECTIVE

JAN.

15¢

A THRILLING
PUBLICATION

the CHINESE
PUZZLE
A Full-Length
Mystery Novel
By ROBERT WALLACE

6

The PHANTOM
DETECTIVE

JAN. 15¢

A THRILLING
PUBLICATION

THE CROOKED MILE RIVER MURDERS
A Full-Length Mystery Novel by ROBERT WALLACE

7

The PHANTOM
DETECTIVE

FALL
20¢

A THRILLING
PUBLICATION

HOMICIDE
TOWN
A Full-Length
Mystery Novel
By ROBERT
WALLACE

THIN VENEER
A Baffling Novelet
By NORMAN A. DANIELS

8

10¢ BLACK BOOK DETECTIVE

FALL ISSUE

MURDER AMONG THE DYING
A Complete Tony Quinn Mystery Novel
By G. WAYMAN JONES

PROTECTIVE ARMOR
An Exciting Story
By NORMAN A. DANIELS

New BLACK BAT MYSTERY NOVEL EVERY ISSUE!

A THRILLING PUBLICATION

9

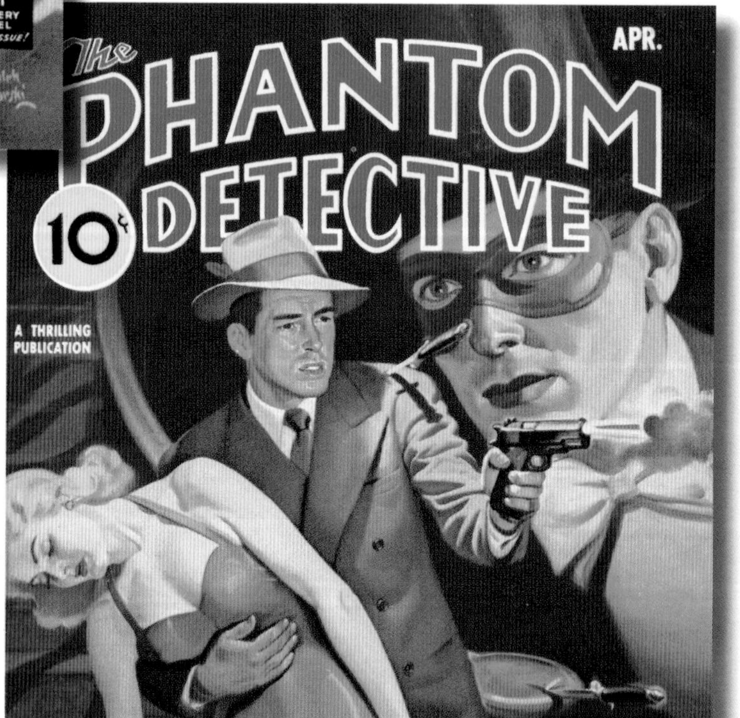

The PHANTOM DETECTIVE

APR.

10¢

A THRILLING PUBLICATION

Let's Give
RED CROSS WAR FUND

THE RUBBER KNIFE Murders
A Complete Book-Length Mystery Novel
By ROBERT WALLACE

10

11

12

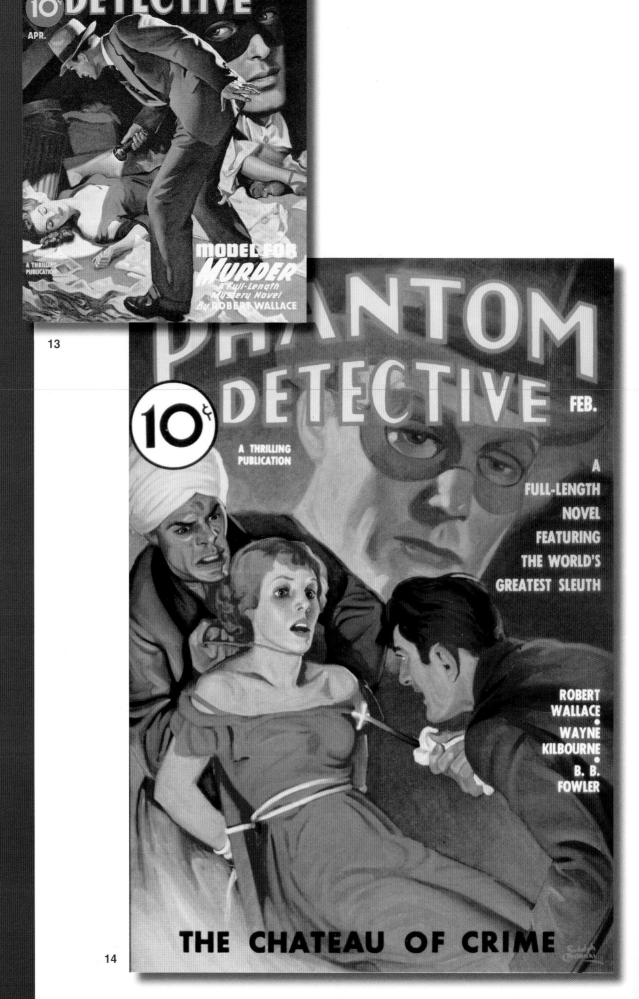

15

16

17

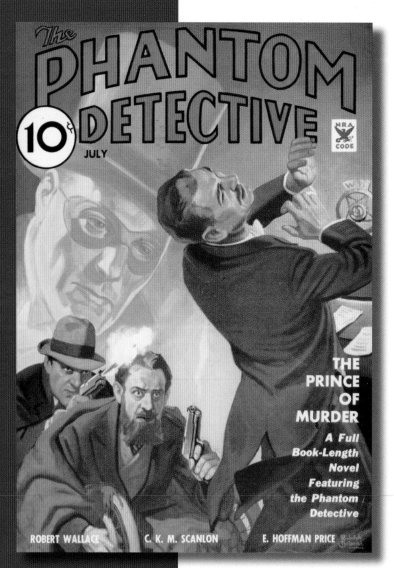

The PHANTOM DETECTIVE

10¢ JULY

NRA CODE

THE PRINCE OF MURDER

A Full Book-Length Novel Featuring the Phantom Detective

ROBERT WALLACE · C. K. M. SCANLON · E. HOFFMAN PRICE

18

The PHANTOM DETECTIVE

MAR. 15¢

A THRILLING PUBLICATION

THE *Clue* OF THE SECOND MURDER

A Full-Length Mystery Novel By ROBERT WALLACE

19

The PHANTOM DETECTIVE

MAY 15¢

The ANGEL OF *DEATH*

A Full-Length Mystery Novel By ROBERT WALLACE

A THRILLING PUBLICATION

20

21

DEALERS
IN
22 DEATH

WOMEN ON THE OFFENSIVE

Image 23
BLACK BOOK DETECTIVE
JUNE 1948
Written by Norman Daniels. 47th Black Bat story.

Image 24
PHANTOM DETECTIVE
MAY 1948
A perfect example of action frozen just after the action took place. 147th Phantom Detective story.

Image 25
PHANTOM DETECTIVE
AUGUST 1936
Phantom Detective's version of Ma Barker? 42nd Phantom Detective story.

Image 26
BLACK BOOK DETECTIVE
WINTER 1944
One of a small handful of covers that the Black Bat is in real action on the cover. Written by Norman Daniels. 27th Black Bat story.

Image 27
BLACK BOOK DETECTIVE
FALL 1950
Written by Norman Daniels. 58th Black Bat story.

Image 28
PHANTOM DETECTIVE
WINTER 1950
156th Phantom Detective story.

Image 29
PHANTOM DETECTIVE
JULY 1947
142nd Phantom Detective story.

Image 30
PHANTOM DETECTIVE
JUNE 1946
136th Phantom Detective story.

23

24

25

26

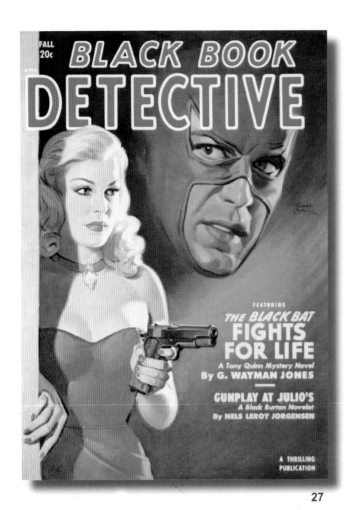

BLACK BOOK DETECTIVE

FALL 20c

FEATURING

THE BLACK BAT **FIGHTS FOR LIFE**

A Tony Quinn Mystery Novel
By G. WAYMAN JONES

GUNPLAY AT JULIO'S
A Black Burton Novelet
By NELS LEROY JORGENSEN

A THRILLING PUBLICATION

27

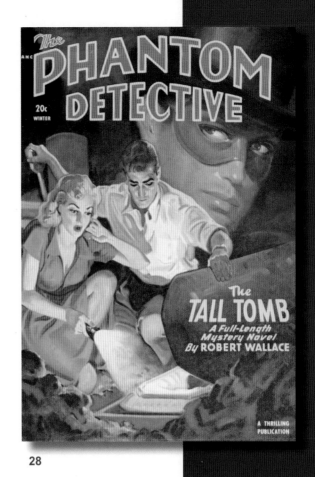

THE PHANTOM DETECTIVE

20c WINTER

The **TALL TOMB**
A Full-Length Mystery Novel
By ROBERT WALLACE

A THRILLING PUBLICATION

28

The PHANTOM DETECTIVE

JULY 15c

MASTERPIECE OF *Murder*
A Full-Length Mystery Novel
By ROBERT WALLACE

A THRILLING PUBLICATION

29

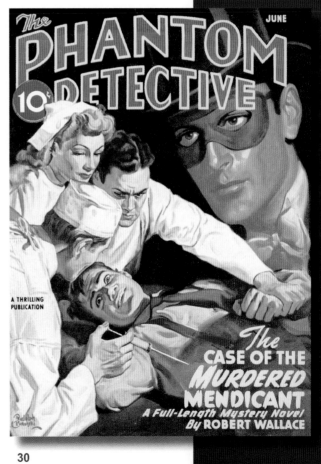

The PHANTOM DETECTIVE

JUNE 10c

The **CASE OF THE** *MURDERED* **MENDICANT**
A Full-Length Mystery Novel
By ROBERT WALLACE

A THRILLING PUBLICATION

30

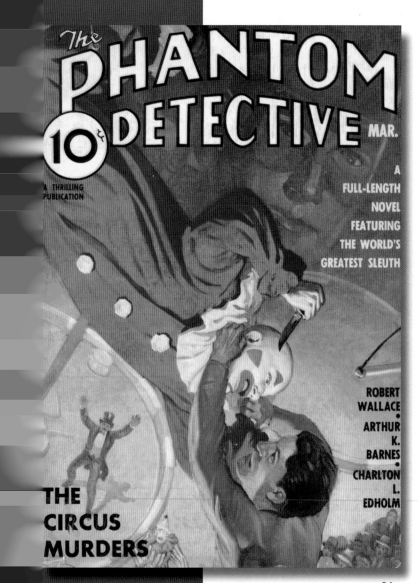

The PHANTOM DETECTIVE
MAR.
10¢
A THRILLING PUBLICATION

A FULL-LENGTH NOVEL FEATURING THE WORLD'S GREATEST SLEUTH

ROBERT WALLACE · ARTHUR K. BARNES · CHARLTON L. EDHOLM

THE CIRCUS MURDERS

31

10¢ BLACK BOOK DETECTIVE
FALL ISSUE
A THRILLING PUBLICATION

GUARDIAN IN BLACK
A Book-Length Novel Featuring the Black Bat, Masked Nemesis of Crime
By G. WAYMAN JONES

32

The PHANTOM DETECTIVE
MAR.
15¢
A THRILLING PUBLICATION

CARTEL OF CRIME
A Full-Length Mystery Novel By ROBERT WALLACE

33

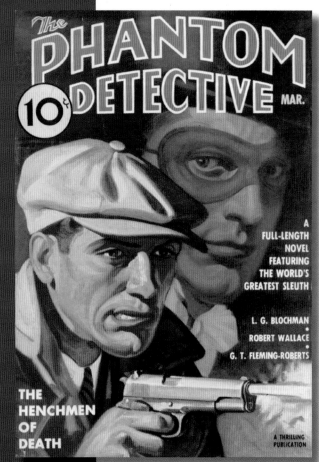

The PHANTOM DETECTIVE
MAR.
10¢

A FULL-LENGTH NOVEL FEATURING THE WORLD'S GREATEST SLEUTH

L. G. BLOCHMAN · ROBERT WALLACE · G. T. FLEMING-ROBERTS

THE HENCHMEN OF DEATH

A THRILLING PUBLICATION

34

The PHANTOM DETECTIVE
FEB.
10¢
A THRILLING PUBLICATION

THE PHANTOM AND THE CURIO MURDERS
A FULL-LENGTH NOVEL FEATURING THE WORLD'S GREATEST SLEUTH

35

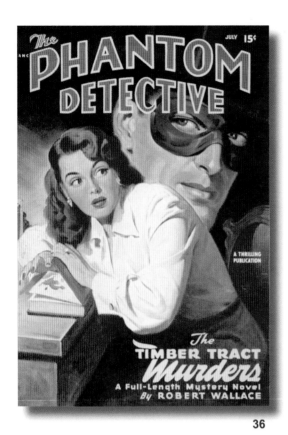

36

37

38

Image 31
**PHANTOM
DETECTIVE
MARCH 1936**
37th Phantom Detective
story.

Image 32
**BLACK BOOK
DETECTIVE
FALL 1943**
Written by Norman
Daniels. 26th Black Bat
story.

Image 33
**PHANTOM
DETECTIVE
MARCH 1947**
140th Phantom Detective
story.

Image 34
**PHANTOM
DETECTIVE
MARCH 1937**
Lead story's author didn't
get top billing. 49th
Phantom Detective story.

Image 35
**PHANTOM
DETECTIVE
FEBRUARY 1941**
96th Phantom Detective
story.

Image 36
**PHANTOM
DETECTIVE
JULY 1948**
148th Phantom Detective
story.

Image 37
**BLACK BOOK
DETECTIVE
FEBRUARY 1947**
Written by Norman
Daniels. 39th Black Bat
story.

Image 38
**PHANTOM
DETECTIVE
DECEMBER 1936**
46th Phantom Detective
story.

**Image 39
PHANTOM
DETECTIVE
JANUARY 1949**
151st Phantom Detective
story.

**Image 40
BLACK BOOK
DETECTIVE
SEPTEMBER 1948**
Written by Norman
Daniels. 48th Black Bat
story.

**Image 41
PHANTOM DETECTIVE
FEBRUARY 1944**
Between a rock and
a hard place. 122nd
Phantom Detective story.

**Image 42
PHANTOM DETECTIVE
FEBRUARY 1946**
134th Phantom Detective
story.

**Image 43
PHANTOM DETECTIVE
MARCH 1949**
152nd Phantom Detective
story.

**Image 44
PHANTOM DETECTIVE
SEPTEMBER 1947**
143rd Phantom Detective
story.

**Image 45
PHANTOM DETECTIVE
NOVEMBER 1936**
45th Phantom Detective
story.

**Image 46
PHANTOM DETECTIVE
NOVEMBER 1948**
150th Phantom Detective
story.

**Image 47
PHANTOM DETECTIVE
NOVEMBER 1947**
144th Phantom Detective
story.

**Image 48
PHANTOM DETECTIVE
FALL 1949**
155th Phantom Detective
story.

39

40

41

42

43

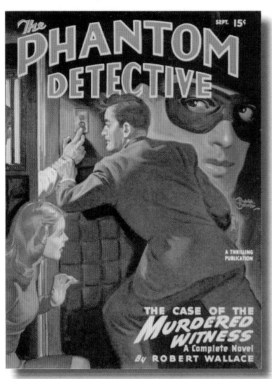

44

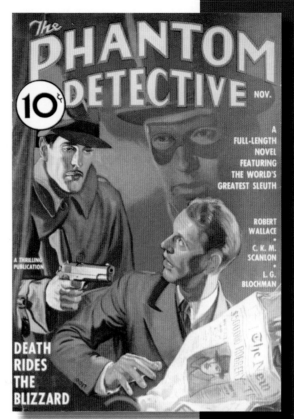

45

46

47

48

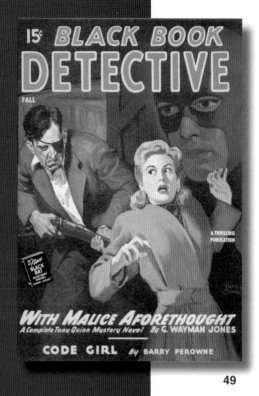

49

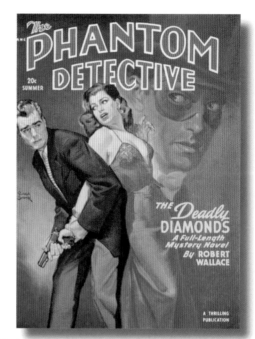

50

51

53

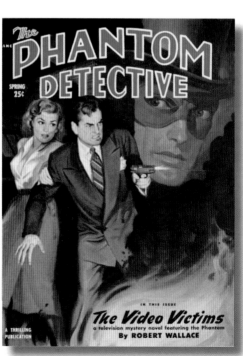

52

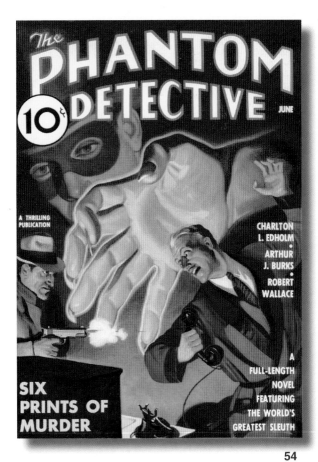

54

55

56

57

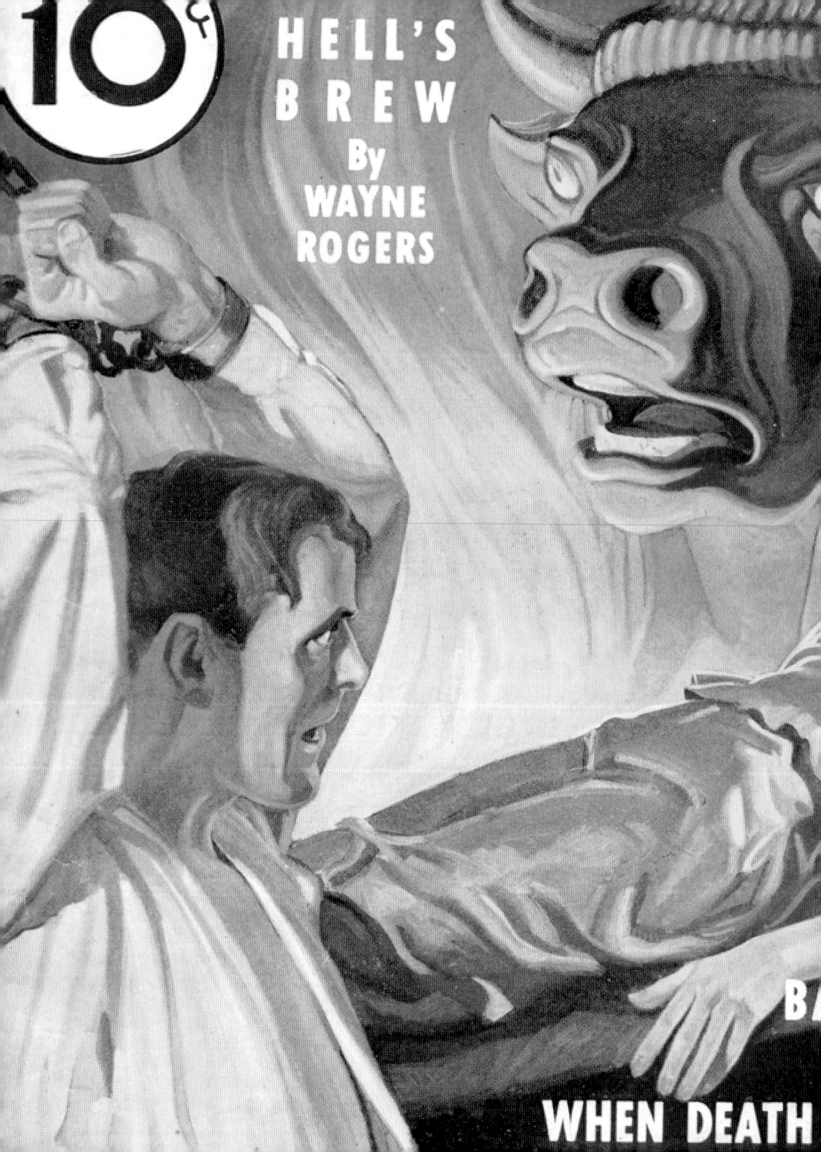

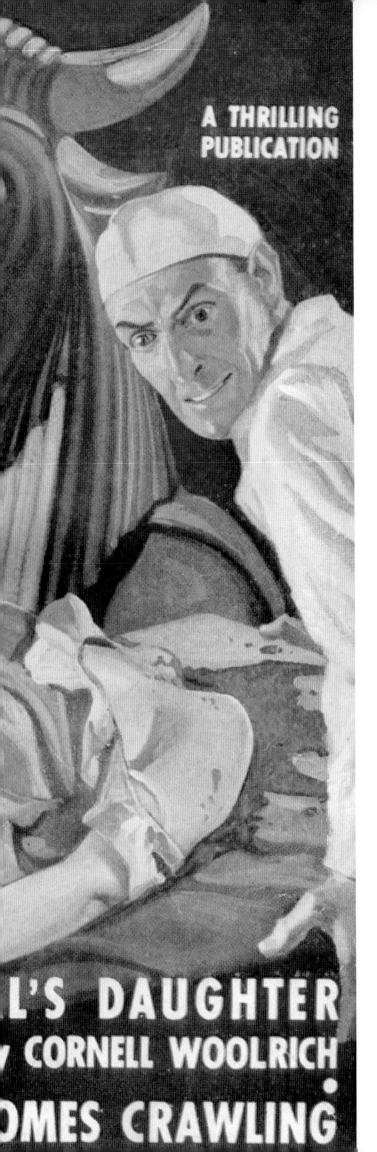

A THRILLING
PUBLICATION

...L'S DAUGHTER

...y CORNELL WOOLRICH

...OMES CRAWLING

GHOULS AND GALS

★ ★ ★ ★ ★

IT WAS early 1932. Harry Steeger, Popular Publication's co-founder and publisher, was looking for a companion for his hit magazine **DIME DETECTIVE**. With just a twist of the name, Steeger came up with **DIME MYSTERY BOOK** and published what was billed as a novel, albeit an abridged version, in a 128-page pulpwood magazine. After a year, the reading public still hadn't warmed to the idea. Steeger realized he needed to cancel the magazine or change the format. Recalling a trip to Paris, Steeger decided to pattern story lines around the theme made popular by The Theatre du Grand Guignol. It was there that patrons viewed ghastly and ghoulish theatrics. Whipping, flaying, dismemberment were a daily diet of the theater and the appalling scenes made quite an impression on Steeger. With another slight twist to the title, **DIME MYSTERY MAGAZINE** was born as the first Weird Menace pulp, and an almost instant hit.

An axiom in the pulp publishing business was if you can't come up with a good idea on your own, you steal it from another and Ned Pines saw the numbers for Popular's **DIME MYSTERY** and their subsequent similar titles, **HORROR STORIES** and **TERROR TALES** and cloned it as **THRILLING MYSTERY**. The formula was to have some impossible gruesome event occur and wrap it up with a "plausible" ending by story's end. Authors like Hugh B. Cave, G. T. Fleming-Roberts, Paul Ernst, Ray Cummings, and Henry Kuttner churned out blood and gore stories by the fistful. Titles like Black Wings of Death, The Thing That Dined on Death, Dragon of the Gobi, Cargo of Horror and Doom That Dwelled Within lurched across newsstands nationwide.

Rudolph Belarski was no stranger to the macabre cover, and dug into this genre with gusto. Decapitations, giant snakes and women being heaved into roaring flames typified the weird menace magazines, and after censorship killed them off, the likes of them wouldn't be seen again until Max Gaines' E.C. Comics horror comics of the 50's.

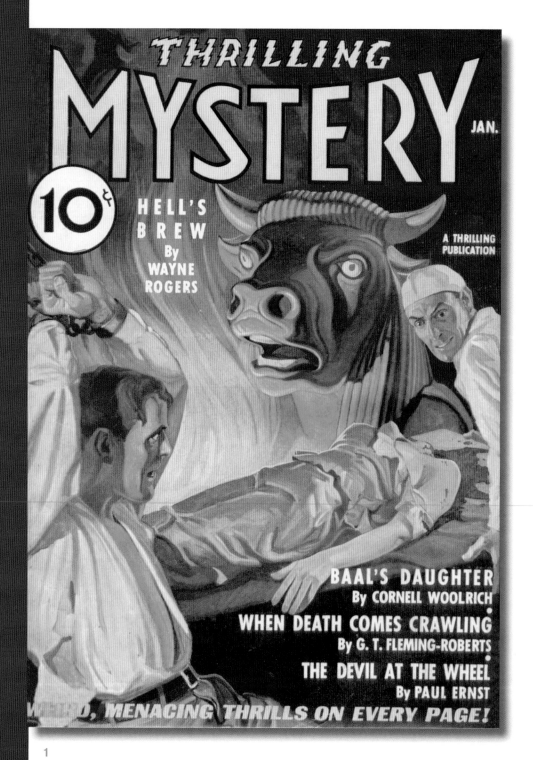

Image 1
THRILLING MYSTERY JANUARY 1936
More gruesome than any comic cover for E.C. Comics.

Image 2
THRILLING MYSTERY JUNE 1943
A strange marriage between weird menace and a hero character the Green Ghost who was moved when his own magazine folded.

Image 3
THRILLING MYSTERY NOVEMBER 1936
The vampire looks to be a combination of The Shadow and Bela Lugosi.

Image 4
THRILLING MYSTERY APRIL 1937
Jack Williamson is better known for his science fiction work than that of his horror material. His weird menace yarns were carried almost exclusively by the Thrilling Group.

Image 5
THRILLING MYSTERY MARCH 1936
Hooded ghouls, not too common on the streets of America in the 30's, yet very popular in the weird menace mags of the day.

1

2

Cover 3

THRILLING MYSTERY

10¢

HELL HOSTEL
A Novelette of Fe...
By WAY...
ROGE...

BLOOD OF MONSTE...
A Novelette of Haunting Ter...
By G. T. FLEMING-ROBER...

HORROR ISLAN...
A Novelette
Satan's Graveyc...
By STEWART ADA...

POWER OF THE SNA...
A Weird Novele...
By HENRY KUTTN...

A THRILLING PUBLICATION

3

Cover 4

THRILLING MYSTERY

10¢

A THRILLING PUBLICATION

DEATH PLAYS...
A Novel...
Subterranean Dread
By HUGH B. CAVE

BRIDE OF THE SHINING DEAD
A Novelette of Midnight Terror
By HAL K. WELLS

HORROR OUT OF THE DEEP
A Spine-Tingling Novelette
By JAMES DUNCAN

SPIDER ISLAND
A Novelette of Doom's Web
By JACK WILLIAMSON

4

Cover 5

THRILLING MYSTERY MAR

10¢
A THRILLING PUBLICATION

FEATURING
THE TWISTED MEN
By HUGH B. CAVE

VENGEANCE OF THE SNAKE-GOD
By JAMES DUNCAN

BLACK MOONLIGHT
By G. T. FLEMING-ROBERTS

BLOOD OF GOLD
By WAYNE ROGERS

AND OTHER STORIES

WEIRD, MENACING THRILLS ON EVERY PAGE!

5

THRILLING MYSTERY

10¢

MAY

DRAGON OF THE GOBI
A Novelet of Desert Terror
By STEWART STERLING

A THRILLING
PUBLICATION

FEATURING
BLACK WINGS
OF DEATH
A Novel of
Masked Horror
By G. T.
FLEMING-ROBERTS

6

THRILLING MYSTERY APR.

10¢

THE ANGRY DEAD
By CHANDLER H. WHIPPLE

A THRILLING
PUBLICATION

MADMAN'S MAGIC
By JAMES DUNCAN

HORROR HOUSE
By RAY CUMMINGS

AND OTHER STORIES

THE THING
THAT DINED ON DEATH
By JOHN H. KNOX

WEIRD, MENACING THRILLS ON EVERY PAGE!

7

THRILLING MYSTERY

10¢

JAN.

A THRILLING
PUBLICATION

FEATURING
THE CYCLOPS' EYE
A Colonel Crum Novelet
By JOHN H. KNOX

NIGHTMARE ISLAND
A Complete Weird Novelet
By H. H. STINSON

WINGS OF
THE BAT
By HENRY
KUTTNER

8

9

10

A THRILLING
PUBLICATION

A POTPOURRI

⭐ ⭐ ⭐ ⭐ ⭐

OF ALL the mainstream genres that pulp publishers produced titles for, Belarski was hired to produce images for nearly all of them.

History has credited Science Fiction as a magazine genre to Hugo Gernsback and his **AMAZING STORIES**. Yet **ARGOSY** was printing fantastic fiction of authors like Edgar Rice Burroughs, Ray Cummings, A. Merritt and others nearly a decade prior to the birth of **AMAZING STORIES**. It was late in the 30's when Belarski was approached to contribute his visions of Tarzan and John Carter of Mars to the covers of **ARGOSY** for stories of these characters. In addition, Belarski painted covers for Thrilling's **STARTLING STORIES** — one of the leading magazines of the era — as well as **THRILLING WONDER**. (Years later art director Bernard Goodman commissioned Belarski to paint covers for the first three issues of the science-fiction digest **ORBIT SCIENCE FICTION**, adding to his science fiction resume.)

Western pulps along with the detective titles were some of the best and most-read magazines of the day. Belarski's Western output was minimal, and the reasons for it unknown. Perhaps it was simply personal taste. Or perhaps it was based in the way art directors chose to utilize his talents for mass market appeal, believing his slick approach and style were better suited to stiff collars, fedoras, straight pant creases and evening gowns than dust, course cloth, ten gallon hats and saddle-worn leather. Whatever the actual reasons, we are more fortunate that between the countless canvases depicting airplanes or automatic handguns that a few Western assignments did emerge from Belarski's studio.

His work for the Thrilling Group included covers for **WEST**, (which by this time had been bought from Doubleday) and **POPULAR WESTERN**. Several cover images were also created for Munsey's **SILVER BUCK WESTERN** and **BIG CHIEF WESTERN**. Early in his career that artist had covers appear on **WILD WEST WEEKLY** as well.

We are also presenting several covers from unknown publications. These images come from Belarski's personal collection of cover proofs and are reproduced here with the hope that someone can help identify them.

The sports-oriented pulp was a small niche market for a publisher. Yet nearly every publisher had his own line of sports magazines. The numbers of copies sold for any publishers' title outside of the Street & Smith's granddaddy SPORT STORY MAGAZINE were minimal. For Belarski, the vast majority of these assignments must have been a snap. With simplistic backgrounds, usually only portraying the simple action of a single figure kicking a football, or perhaps fielding a baseball the artist could not have spent more than a day in producing them.

The one exception to this was the war/sport story theme covers which appeared during World War II. War theme backgrounds highlighted by a sport figure in the foreground were all the rage, and Belarski didn't disappoint buyers with a few versions of his own.

Image 1
POPULAR SPORTS
MAGAZINE
WINTER 1945

Image 2
EXCITING SPORTS
SUMMER 1946

Image 3
ARGOSY
APRIL 16 1938
ARGOSY's diversity was legendary as evident that it published stories from aviation to sports and everything else in between.

Image 4
ARGOSY
JUNE 3 1939
Judson Philips was also known as the author of the Park Avenue Hunt Club detective series.

Image 5
POPULAR WESTERN
MAY 1944

Image 6
SILVER BUCK
WESTERN
NOVEMBER 1940
One of a small number of titles Munsey published centered around a single character. Western hero pulps were fairly uncommon as well.

Image 7
THRILLING SPORTS
DECEMBER 1946

Image 8
EXCITING FOOTBALL
WINTER 1946
An interesting World War II tactic of superimposing a warrior's previous life over his current career.

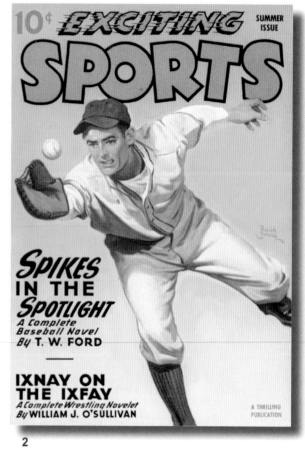

1

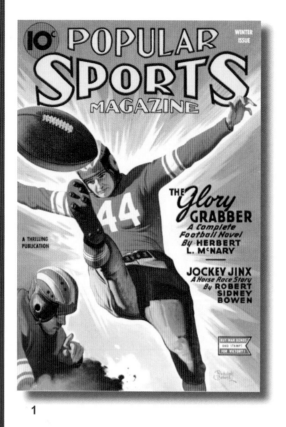

2

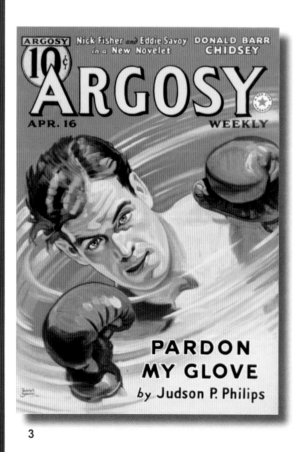

3

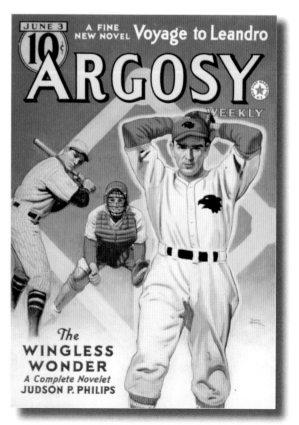

4

COMPLETE QUICK-TRIGGER STORIES

10¢

POPULAR WESTERN
MAY

BUY WAR BONDS AND STAMPS FOR VICTORY!

A THRILLING PUBLICATION

Painted Trail
An Exciting Novelet
By **JOHNSTON McCULLEY**

RUN, SHEEP, RUN
A Range War Novelet
By **SAMUEL MINES**

THE CACTUS PHANTOM
A Sheriff Blue Steele Novelet
By **TOM GUNN**

5

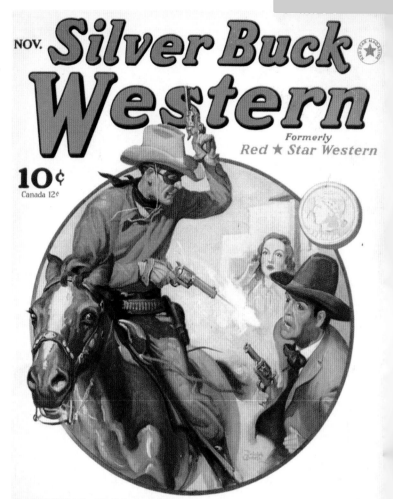

NOV. **Silver Buck**

Western
Formerly
Red ★ Star Western

10¢
Canada 12¢

WHILE SIX-GUNS FLAME, SILVER BUCK, THE SCOURGE OF THE LAWLESS, SEEKS THE SECRET OF
PLUNDER PLATEAU
A new, complete and thrilling novel by James P. Olsen

6

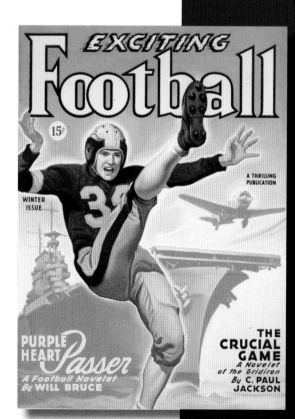

THRILLING
SPORTS
15¢
DEC.

THRILLS IN SPORTS
By **JACK KOFOED**

A THRILLING PUBLICATION

CRAZY FOR TROUBLE
A Football Novelet
By **WILLIAM J. O'SULLIVAN**

UNBEATEN SEASON
A Gridiron Novel
By **TRACY MASON**

7

EXCITING
Football
15¢

WINTER ISSUE

A THRILLING PUBLICATION

PURPLE HEART *Passer*
A Football Novelet
By **WILL BRUCE**

THE CRUCIAL GAME
A Novelet of the Gridiron
By **C. PAUL JACKSON**

8

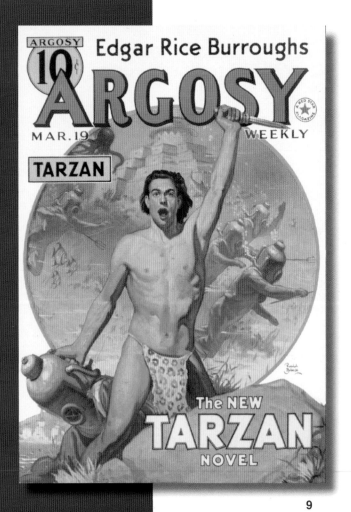

9

10

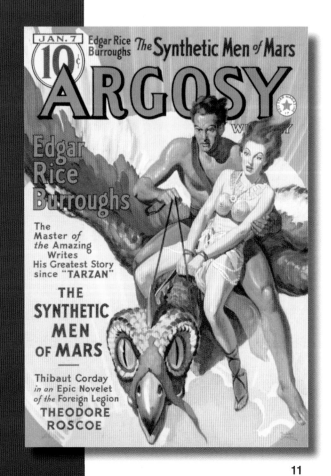

11

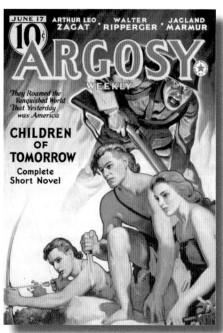

12

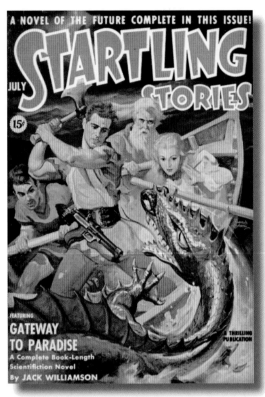

13

14

15

16

Image 17
WESTERN SCENE 1
UNKNOWN
MAGAZINE
These western cover proofs had no logos therefore impossible to know which publisher or title they might have been used on.

Image 18
WESTERN SCENE 2
UNKNOWN
MAGAZINE

Image 19
WESTERN SCENE 3
UNKNOWN
MAGAZINE

Image 20
BIG CHIEF WESTERN
DECEMBER 1940
The White Eagle, a white Indian as hero, a very rare example of this type of story. BIG CHIEF WESTERN was a very short run title.

Image 21
WEST
MAY 1944
Zorro, although not in this issue started in ARGOSY and wrapped up nearly 30 years later in WEST.

Image 22
WEST
NOVEMBER 1943

Image 23
WILD WEST WEEKLY
NOVEMBER 2 1935
Belarski had very little work with Street & Smith. This could very well be the only cover for WILD WEST WEEKLY as this author is unaware of any other with cover art by Rudolph Belarski.

17

18

19

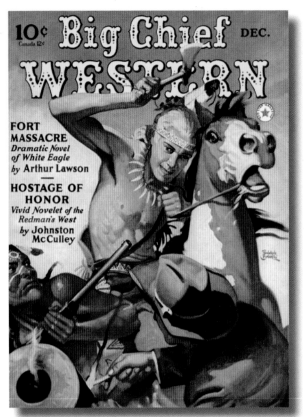

20

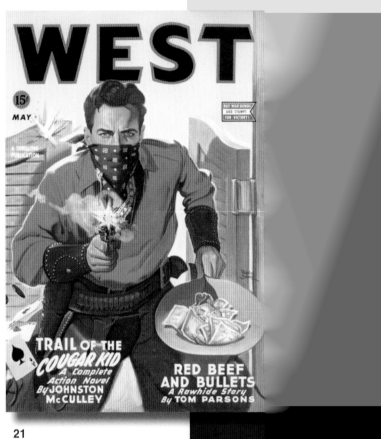

21

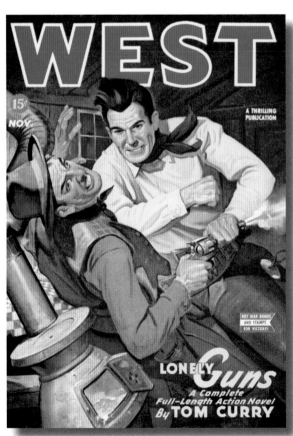

22

23

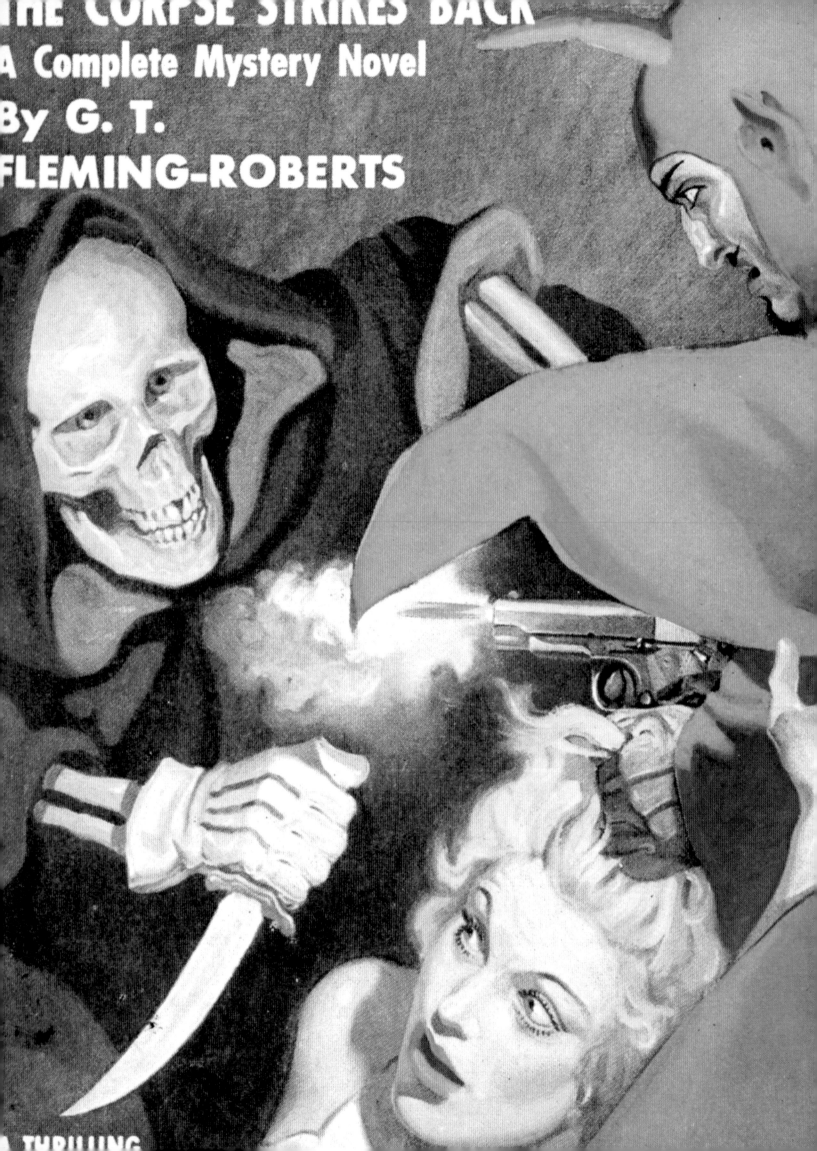

THE CORPSE STRIKES BACK
A Complete Mystery Novel
By G. T.
FLEMING-ROBERTS

THRILLING

DEM BONES..
DEM BONES

★ ★ ★ ★ ★

LIVING SKELETONS. Walking boneyards. Specters of dread and doom. Fantastic images designed to evoke an emotional response, to shock and titillate the reader. Rudolph Belarski's use of these skeletal remnants span from the aviation titles through the hero pulps, from the detective magazines to where one would expect them to be — on a weird menace cover.

Belarski's beady-eyed hooded figure of death jumps off the printed page like a thunderbolt. It commands your attention. This cover motif, apparently a favorite of Belarski and popularized through frequent use by him was not a unique idea but used by several of the great pulp artists. George Rozen utilized this theme several times for covers of **THE SHADOW** and other pulp titles as well. A dancing skeleton turned up on a **COMPLETE DETECTIVE** cover by Norman Saunders. Expert aviation artist Frederick Blakeslee even had animated corpses piloting World War I aircraft in dogfights against **G-8 AND HIS BATTLE ACES**. But there is something about Belarski's renditions that transcends the approach to the subject use by others. There is nothing comical about them. His remain haunting to this day.

✪ ✪ ✪ ✪ ✪

For Rudolph Belarski, the constant theme he strove for with his art was to involve the reader in the action. The covers for pulp magazines were designed to attract any potential buyer long before they knew what the inside contents held. Fantastic images of bold color, and outrageous action, all screamed from the newsstands of Depression-era America. The magazine publisher knew that their audience was looking for escape. The pulpwood editor knew better than any that action and adventure counted more than an intricate plot. The art director quickly learned which artists would sell more magazines. It was a cold hard fact that some publishers could not, or would not pay their authors for stories, but the art was bought and the artist was paid up front because it would be the cover that sold the magazine — not the half-cent per word starving unknown author.

Rudolph Belarski's career lasted through a depression, a world war, and the eventual death of the pulp market itself. He continued producing new art for magazines and covers for the growing paperback industry, but the best work of his career was with those 128 page untrimmed wonders known as the pulps.

FIGHTING DAREDEVILS OF TODAY'S WAR

AIR WAR

A THRILLING PUBLICATION

10¢

SUMMER ISSUE

THE THIRTEENTH
Mission
An Army Air Novelet
By NORMAN A.
DANIELS

FAREWELL
TO ZEROS
A Navy
Air Novelet
By LT. FRANK
JOHNSON

BUY WAR BONDS
AND STAMPS
FOR VICTORY!

1

N STORIES OF THE F. B. I.

G-MEN
DETECTIVE

A THRILLING
PUBLICATION

FEATURING

ASSASSINS
IN
Celluloid
A Dan Fowler Mystery Novel
By STEWART STERLING
—
LOSERS WEEPERS
A Suspenseful Novelet
By EDWARD RONNS

THRILLING
PUBLICATION

2

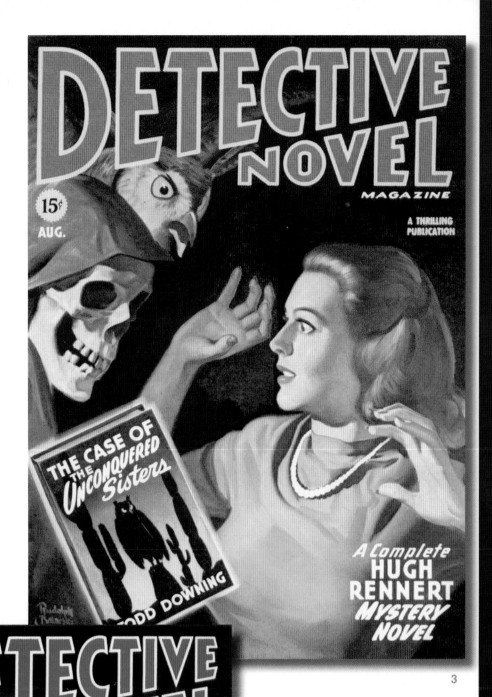

3

4

Image 1
AIR WAR
SUMMER 1944
Norman Daniels appears
both in his own name and
that of a house name of
Lt. Frank Johnson.

Image 2
G-MEN DETECTIVE
WINTER 1950
Murder by cigarette?

Image 3
DETECTIVE NOVEL
MAGAZINE
AUGUST 1946
Inclusion of the original
dull hardback book cover
art hardly takes away
from the superior Belarski
composition.

Image 4
DETECTIVE NOVEL
MAGAZINE
JULY 1947
Death signals for silence.

Image 5
DETECTIVE FICTION WEEKLY
NOVEMBER 20 1937
Author John K. Butler went from selling stories to the pulpwood magazines to Hollywood movies. Never having a book published of his stories in his lifetime, Adventure House published the first with AT THE STROKE OF MIDNIGHT.

Image 6
POPULAR DETECTIVE
MAY 1947
Robert Sidney Bowen wrote for sports pulps, aviation, western and even hero pulps. An all-around author who sold for nearly every pulp publisher.

Image 7
MYSTERY BOOK MAGAZINE
WINTER 1948
Well before Roger Moore portrays The Saint on television, Leslie Charteris' character was published in many different pulp titles.

Image 8
PHANTOM DETECTIVE
MAY 1936
39th Phantom Detective story.

Image 9
POPULAR DETECTIVE
DECEMBER 1937
Ray Cummings had a limited number of continuing detective characters, yet is better known for his science fiction stories in the early 20's for ARGOSY.

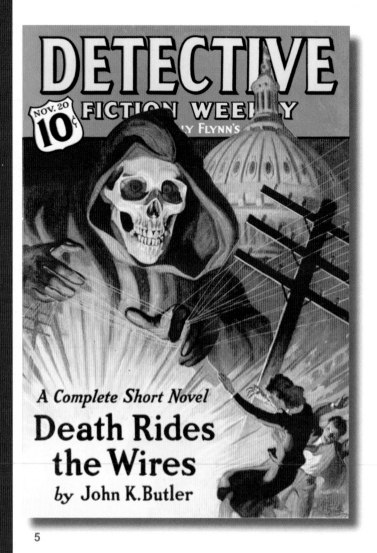

5

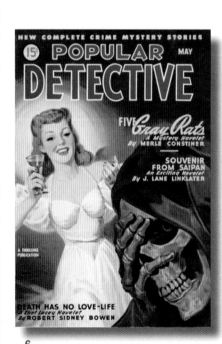

6

7

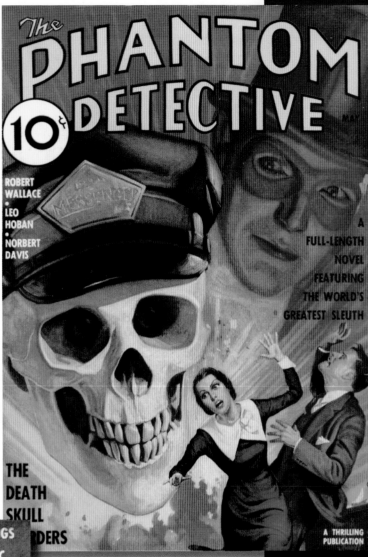

The PHANTOM DETECTIVE

10¢

ROBERT
WALLACE
•
LEO
HOBAN
•
NORBERT
DAVIS

MAY

A
FULL-LENGTH
NOVEL
FEATURING
THE WORLD'S
GREATEST SLEUTH

THE
DEATH
SKULL
RDERS

A THRILLING
PUBLICATION

8

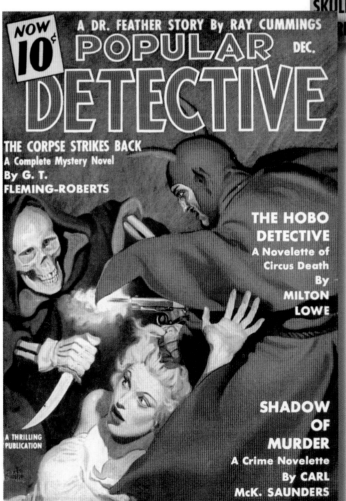

A DR. FEATHER STORY By RAY CUMMINGS

NOW
10¢

POPULAR DETECTIVE

DEC.

THE CORPSE STRIKES BACK
A Complete Mystery Novel
By G. T.
FLEMING-ROBERTS

THE HOBO
DETECTIVE
A Novelette of
Circus Death
By
MILTON
LOWE

SHADOW
OF
MURDER
A Crime Novelette
By CARL
McK. SAUNDERS

A THRILLING
PUBLICATION

9

10

11

13

12

14

Image 10
THRILLING
DETECTIVE
JANUARY 1936
Laurence Donovan wrote
a number of detective
stories, as well as one of
the ghost writers for DOC
SAVAGE author Lester
Dent.

Image 11
THRILLING
DETECTIVE
APRIL 1948
Bellem's Nick Ransom,
although a blood brother
of Dan Turner, has yet to
garner the same attention
as SPICY DETECTIVE's
favorite Hollywood Private
Eye.

Image 12
PHANTOM
DETECTIVE
AUGUST 1946
137th Phantom Detective
story.

Image 13
THRILLING
DETECTIVE
OCTOBER 1948
Post World War II pulps
had a nearly all-new
lineup of authors, as most
of the previous best-sell-
ers had either moved on
to the slicks, radio or the
movies.

Image 14
POPULAR
DETECTIVE
DECEMBER 1945
Demonic Santa Claus?
Can't bring yourself to
give this guy a kiss under
the mistletoe?

**Image 15
THRILLING
DETECTIVE
DECEMBER 1947**
Even post World War II
titles had some all-stars
appear. This issue had a
number of old hands with
Carroll John Daly, Louis
L'Amour and William
O'Sullivan.

**Image 16
THRILLING MYSTERY
MARCH 1937**
Featured author Wyatt
Blassingame's brother,
Lurton Blassingame, was
one of pulp magazines
largest and most influen-
tial agents.

**Image 17
THRILLING MYSTERY
NOVEL MAGAZINE
NOVEMBER 1946**
He might not have an
axe to grind, but the
knife seems to be good
enough.

**Image 18
WINGS
MARCH 1935**
In this author's opinion
possibly one of the most
awe inspiring covers ever
to appear on WINGS.

15

16

17

18

INDEX

Rudolph Belarski (1900-1983)
A Bibliography of Pulp Magazine Art
compiled by Tom Roberts with a nod of thanks to Albert Tonik.

ACE-HIGH MAGAZINE
[Dell Publishing Co., Inc.]
1934, September
1934, October

ACES
[Fiction House]
1929, October
1929, November
1929, December
1930, March
1930, April
1930, May
1930, June
1930, July
1930, September
1930, October
1930, December
1931, January
1931, July
1931, August
1931, September
1931, October
1931, November
1931, December
1932, January
1932, February
1932, March
1932, April
1932, May
1932, June
1932, July,
1932, August
1932, September
1932, October
1932, November
1932, December
1933, August
1937, Spring
1937, Winter
1938, Spring
1939, Spring
1940, Winter

ACE-HIGH MAGAZINE
[Dell Publishing Co., Inc]
1934, October

AIR STORIES
[Fictioneers, Inc./Fiction House]
1930, January
1930, April
1930, July
1930, October
1930, December
1931, July
1931, August
1931, September
1931, October
1931, November
1931, December
1932, January
1932, February
1932, March
1932, April

AIRPLANE STORIES
[Ramar Reviews]
1929, March, (Vol. 1, #1)
1929, April
1929, May
1929, June
1929, July
1929, August
1929, September
1929, October
1929, November
1930, January

1930, February
1930, March
1930, April
1930, May
1930, June
1930, August
1930, September
1930, October
1930, November
1930, December

AIR WAR
[Standard Magazines, Inc./Thrilling Group]
1941, Spring
1941, Summer
1941, Fall
1942, March
1942, Spring
1942, Summer
1944, Spring

ALL-AMERICAN FICTION
[Frank A. Munsey Co.]
1937, December
1938, February
1938, March/April
1938, May/June
1938, July/August
1938, September/October

THE AMERICAN EAGLE
[Standard Magazines, Inc./Thrilling Group]
1941, August
1942, Winter
1942, February
1942, April
1942, Fall
1943, Winter

AMERICAN EAGLES
1943, Spring

ARGOSY
[Frank A. Munsey Co.]
1935, July 6
1936, September 12
1937, March 2
1937, April 24
1937, May 15
1937, May 29
1937, June 26
1937, July 17
1937, August 28
1937, September 18
1937, November 13
1937, November 27
1937, December 11
1938, January 1
1938, January 8
1938, January 22
1938, February 19
1938, March 19
1938, March 30
1938, April 16
1938, April 23
1938, May 7
1938, May 28
1938, June 4
1938, June 18
1938, July 2
1938, July 9
1938, July 23
1938, August 20
1938, September 3
1938, September 17
1938, September 24
1938, October 22
1938, November 5

1938, November 12
1938, November 19
1938, November 26
1938, December 17
1939, January 7
1939, February 4
1939, March 4
1939, March 11
1939, April 1
1939, April 22
1939, April 29
1939, May 6
1939, May 20
1939, May 27
1939, June 3
1939, June 17
1939, June 24
1939, July 1
1939, July 15
1939, July 22
1939, July 29
1939, August 5
1939, August 12
1939, September 2
1939, September 9
1939, September 23
1939, October 14
1939, October 28
1939, November 4
1939, November 18
1939, December 2
1939, December 9
1939, December 23
1939, December 30
1940, January 13
1940, January 20
1940, January 27
1940, February 24
1940, March 9
1940, March 23
1940, March 30
1940, April 6
1940, April 20
1940, May 4
1940, May 11
1940, May 18
1940, May 25
1940, June 1
1940, June 8
1940, June 22
1940, July 13
1940, July 27

ARMY NAVY FLYING STORIES
[Standard Publishing Co., Inc.]
1942, March, , (V 1, #1)
1942, Fall
1943, Winter
1943, Spring
1943, Summer
1943, Fall

BATTLE ACES
[Popular Publications, Inc.]
1930, November
1931, January

BIG CHIEF WESTERN
[Frank A. Munsey Co./Red Star]
1940, December

BLACK ACES
[Fiction House]
1932, March

BLACK BOOK DETECTIVE
[Standard Magazines, Inc./Thrilling

Group]
1943, Fall
1944, Winter
1944, Spring
1944, Summer
1944, Fall
1945, Fall
1946, Winter
1946, Spring
1946, Summer
1946, Fall
1947, February
1947, April
1947, June
1947, August
1947, October
1947, December
1948, February
1948, April
1948, June
1948, September
1948, November
1949, January
1949, March
1949, Summer - Pop. Lib. #382
1949, Fall
1950, Winter
1950, Spring
1950, Summer
1950, Fall

BLACK MASK
[Pro-Distributors, Inc]
1935, August
1935, October

CAPTAIN FUTURE
[Standard Magazines, Inc./Thrilling Group]
1942, Summer
1942, Fall

CAVALIER CLASSICS
[Frank A. Munsey Co./Red Star]
1940, Summer
1940, November

COMPLETE AVIATION NOVEL MAGAZINE
[Ramar Reviews]
1929, August

DETECTIVE FICTION WEEKLY
[Frank A. Munsey Co./Red Star]
1937, July 3
1937, August 28
1937, September 11
1937, October 2
1937, October 16
1937, November 20
1937, December 25
1938, March 12
1938, March 19
1938, April 9
1938, May 7
1938, May 21
1938, July 2
1938, July 30
1938, August 13
1938, September 17
1938, October 8
1938, October 29
1938, December 3
1939, January 14
1939, January 28
1939, February 18
1939, March 18
1939, April 8

1939, October 21
1939, October 28
1939, November 18

DETECTIVE MYSTERY NOVEL MAGAZINE
[Standard Magazines, Inc./Thrilling Group]
1947, Summer
1947, Fall
1948, Winter
1948, Spring
1948, Summer
1948, Fall
1949, Winter
1949, Spring
1949, Summer

DETECTIVE NOVEL MAGAZINE
[Standard Magazines, Inc./Thrilling Group]
1944, August - Pop. Lib. #201
1944, October
1944, December
1945, February
1945, August
1945, October
1945, December
1946, February
1946, April
1946, June
1946, August
1946, November
1947, January
1947, Winter
1947, March
1947, May
1947, July
1947, September
1947, November
1948, January
1948, March
1948, Spring
1948, Fall
1949, Winter
1949, February
1949, Spring - Pop. Lib. #302
1949, Summer
1949, Fall

DETECTIVE NOVELS MAGAZINE
[Standard Magazines, Inc./Thrilling Group]
1943, Dec. - Pop. Lib. #211
1944, February
1944, April

DOUBLE DETECTIVE
[Frank A. Munsey Co./Red Star]
1938, January
1938, March
1938, July
1938, August
1938, October
1938, November
1938, December
1939, January
1939, February
1939, March
1939, April
1939, May
1939, June
1939, July
1939, August

1939, October 21
1939, October 28
1939, November 18

1940, September
EXCITING FOOTBALL
[Better Publications, Inc./Thrilling Group]
1946, Winter

EXCITING NAVY STORIES
[Better Publications, Inc./Thrilling Group]
1942, April, (Vol. 1, No. 1)
1943, Winter

EXCITING SPORTS
[Better Publications, Inc./Thrilling Group]
1946, Winter

5 DETECTIVE NOVELS MAGAZINE
[Standard Magazines, Inc./Thrilling Group]
1949, November
1950, Winter
1950, Summer
1950, Fall
1951, Summer

FOREIGN LEGION ADVENTURES
[Frank A. Munsey Co./ Red Star]
1940, October

GIANT DETECTIVE
[Standard Magazines, Inc./Thrilling Group]
1950, Fall
1951, Winter
1951, Spring

G-MEN
[Standard Magazines, Inc./Thrilling Group]
1936, January
1936, December
1937, February
1937, November

G-MEN DETECTIVE
1944, Winter
1944, Spring
1944, Summer
1945, Winter
1946, Winter
1946, February
1946, April
1946, Summer
1946, Fall
1947, January
1947, March
1947, May
1947, July
1947, September
1947, November
1948, January
1948, March - Pop. Lib. #344
1948, May
1948, July
1948, November
1949, January
1949, February
1949, March - Pop. Lib. #292
1949, Spring
1949, Summer
1949, Fall
1950, Winter
1950, Spring
1950, Summer
1950, Fall

GEORGE BRUCE'S AIR NOVELS
[Glen-Kel Publishing Co., Inc./Fiction House]
1931

LARIAT STORY MAGAZINE
[Real Adventures Pub. Co./Fiction House]
1934, June

LONE EAGLE, THE
[Better Publications, Inc./Thrilling Group]
1937, February
1937, August
1940, December
1941, April

MYSTERY BOOK MAGAZINE
[Best Publications, Inc./Thrilling Group]
1947, Fall
1948, Winter
1948, Spring
1948, Summer
1948, Fall
1949, Winter
1949, Feb. - Pop. Lib. #276
1949, Spring
1949, Summer - Pop. Lib. #293
1949, Fall
1950, Spring
1950, Summer

THE PHANTOM DETECTIVE
[Standard Magazines, Inc./Thrilling Group]
1935, March
1935, April
1935, July
1935, August
1935, September
1935, November
1935, December
1936, January
1936, February
1936, March
1936, April
1936, May
1936, June
1936, July
1936, August
1936, September
1936, October
1936, November
1936, December
1937, January
1937, March
1937, April
1937, May
1937, July
1937, August
1937, September
1937, October
1938, March
1938, June
1941, February
1942, July
1942, October
1943, October
1943, December
1944, February
1944, April
1944, August
1944, October
1944, December
1945, February
1945, December
1946, February
1946, April
1946, June
1946, August
1946, November
1947, January

1947, March
1947, May
1947, July
1947, September
1947, November
1948, January
1948, March - Pop. Lib. #194
1948, May
1948, July
1948, September
1948, November
1949, January
1949, March
1949, Spring
1949, Summer
1949, Fall
1950, Winter
1950, Spring
1950, Summer - Pop. Lib. #362
1950, Fall
1951, Winter
1951, Spring

POPULAR DETECTIVE
[Standard Magazines, Inc./Thrilling Group]
1935, December
1936, November
1937, June
1937, December
1940, December
1941, April
1944, April
1944, October
1945, December
1946, June
1946, August
1946, November
1947, January
1947, May
1947, August
1947, September
1947, November
1948, January
1948, March
1948, May
1948, Sept. - Pop. Lib. #227
1948, November
1949, January
1949, March
1949, May
1949, July
1949, September
1949, November
1950, January
1950, March
1950, May
1950, July
1950, September
1950, November
1951, January
1951, July

POPULAR SPORTS MAGAZINE
[Better Publications, Inc./Thrilling Group]
1945, Winter

POPULAR WESTERN
[Beacon Magazines, Inc./Thrilling Group]
1944, May

RAF ACES
[Standard Magazines, Inc./Thrilling Group]
1941, August, (V1, # 1)
1942, Winter
1942, March
1942, Spring
1942, Summer
1942, Fall
1943, Winter
1943, Spring
1944, Winter

RED STAR ADVENTURES
[Frank A Munsey Co./Red Star]
1940, June (Vol. 1, No. 1)
1940, August

SEA NOVEL MAGAZINE
[Frank A Munsey Co./Red Star]
1940, November, (V1,# 1)

SILVER BUCK WESTERN
[Frank A Munsey Co./Red Star]
1940, November (V 1,# 1)
1941, January

SKY FIGHTERS
[William L. Mayer & Co.]
1941, January
1942, May
1942, July
1942, November
1943, March
1943, May
1943, September
1943, November
1944, March
1944, Summer

STARLING STORIES
[Standard Magazines, Inc./Thrilling Group]
1941, May
1941, July
1941, September
1941, November
1942, January
1942, September
1943, January
1943, March
1947, March

STRANGE STORIES
[Standard Magazines, Inc./Thrilling Group]
1939, February
1940, April

TERENCE X. O'LEARY'S WAR BIRDS
[Dell Publishing Co., Inc.]
1935, March (V1, #1)
1935, April
1935, June

THRILLING ADVENTURES
[Standard Magazines, Inc./Thrilling Group]
1936, January
1936, May
1936, June
1936, July
1936, September
1936, October
1936, November
1936, December
1937, January
1937, March
1937, May
1937, June
1937, October
1940, April
1940, June
1940, July
1940, September
1940, October
1940, November
1941, January
1941, March
1941, April
1941, May
1941, June
1941, July
1941, September
1941, November
1942, January
1942, February

1942, April
1942, June
1942, July
1942, October
1942, November
1943, January
1943, November

THRILLING DETECTIVE
[Standard Magazines, Inc./Thrilling Group]
1936, January
1937, March
1940, August
1940, November
1940, December
1941, January
1941, March
1941, May
1941, September
1941, December
1942, March
1942, October
1944, January
1944, June
1944, July
1944, October
1944, December
1945, January
1945, November
1946, January
1946, March
1946, May
1946, July
1946, September
1946, October
1946, December
1947, February
1947, April
1947, June
1947, August - Pop. Lib. #188
1947, October
1947, December
1948, April
1948, June
1948, August
1948, Oct. - Pop. Lib. #317
1948, December
1949, February
1949, April
1949, June
1949, August - Pop. Lib. #227
1949, October
1949, December
1950, February
1950, April
1950, October
1951, April

THRILLING MYSTERY
[Standard Magazines, Inc./Thrilling Group]
1935? December, (V1,#1)
1936, January
1936, March
1936, April
1936, June
1936, July
1936, September
1936, October
1936, November
1936, December
1937, March
1937, April
1937, May
1937, June
1940, May
1941, January
1942, March
1944, Winter
1944, Spring

THRILLING MYSTERY NOVEL MAGAZINE

1944, December
1945, Spring
1945, Summer
1945, Fall
1945, November
1946, January
1946, March
1946, May - Pop. Lib. #155
1946, Summer
1946, November
1947, January
1947, March - Pop. Lib. #174
1947, May

THRILLING SPORTS
[Standard Magazines, Inc./Thrilling Group]
1946, December
1947, Winter

THRILLING WONDER STORIES
[Better Publications, Inc./Thrilling Group]
1941, August
1941, October
1942, February
1942, August
1942, December
1944, Winter
1944, Spring
1944, Fall

2 DETECTIVE MYSTERY NOVELS MAGAZINE
[Standard Magazines, Inc./Thrilling Group]
1949, Spring
1950, Summer
1950, Fall
1951, Winter

WAR ACES
[Dell Publishing Co., Inc.]
1931, October
1931, November

WAR BIRDS
[Dell Publishing Co., Inc.]
1928, May
1928, September
1930, September
1931, October
1931, December
1932, May
1932, July
1932, October
1933, May
1933, October
1933, December
1934, February
1934, March
1934, April
1934, May
1934, June
1934, July
1934, August
1934, September
1934, October
1934, November
1934, December
1935, January
1935, February
1935, April

WAR NOVELS
[Dell Publishing Co., Inc.]
1928, May
1928, June
1928, July
1928, September
1928, October

WAR STORIES
[Dell Publishing Co., Inc.]
1928, June 7
1928, June 21
1928, August 16
1928, September 13
1928, October 11

1928, November 22
1928, December 20
1929, January 17
1929, February 28
1929, March 14
1929, March 28
1929, August 29
1929, November 21
1930, April 10

WEST
[Better Publications, Inc.]
1943 November
1944 March
1944 May

WESTERN ROMANCES
[Dell Publishing Co., Inc.]
1934 April

WESTERN ROUND-UP
[William H. Cook Publishing Co., Inc.]
1934, July (Vol. 1, No. 1)

WILD WEST WEEKLY
[Street & Smith Publishing Co., Inc.]
1935, November 2

WINGS
[Wings Publishing Co., Inc./Fiction House]
1930, March
1930, April
1930, August
1930, December
1931, January
1931, June
1931, July
1931, August
1931, October
1931, November
1931, December
1932, January
1932, February
1932, March
1932, April
1932, May
1932, June
1932, July
1932, August
1932, September
1932, October
1932, November
1932, Dec
1933, June
1933, Dec/1934, Jan.
1934, Feb./Mar.
1934, April/May
1934, July
1934, September
1934, October
1934, November
1935, January
1935, February
1935, March
1935, April/May
1936, Spring
1936, Fall
1936, Winter
1937, Spring
1937, Summer
1937, Fall
1937, Winter
1938, Spring
1938, Summer
1938, Fall
1939, Winter
1939, Spring
1939, Summer
1939, Fall
1940, Winter

WONDER STORY ANNUAL
[Standard Magazines Inc.]
1951